Vanilla Javascript Projects - From Beginner to Advanced

ISBN: 9798878051323

Table of Contents

1. Introduction...5

2. Temperature Conversion...7

3. Temperature Conversion (version 2)..............................11

4. Color Picker...15

5. Color Picker (version 2)..21

6. Alarm clock...27

7. Todo List..33

8. Todo List (version 2)..39

9. Todo List (version 3)..43

10. Form validation 49

11. Appointments list 57

12. Appointments list (version 2) 69

13. Appointments list (version 3) 81

14. Appointments list (version 4) 87

15. Expense tracker 105

16. Currencies portfolio 117

17. OpenLayer maps with meteo information 125

18. Product list with infinite scroll.................................133

19. Netflix clone..139

20. Book list with Node.js API 151

21. Master-detail form (Angular clone) 163

22. Master-detail form (React clone) 171

23. PacMan game 177

1. Introduction

Before embarking on creating our projects, it would be a good idea to discuss about how to create a project, how to run it and also how to debug it.

Development

The projects in this book were developed using Visual Studio Code (https://code.visualstudio.com), a free Integrated Development Environment (IDE) from Microsoft. We can also use other IDEs, such Eclipse or WebStorm.

Working with VS Code is simple. We should create a folder in our drive where we will place all our code. Then we can select *Open Folder* from the *File* menu to open the specific folder. The files contained in this folder will all be part of the project.

Running

For simple web pages, it is sufficient to double-click on the HTML file to run it. The web page will open in the default web browser, and it will be ready to play with. We can also install the *Live Server* extension for VS Code, that runs a small web server inside VS Code. When we will learn about webpack and vite, we will use their own servers for development.

For each project, there will be exact instructions on how to run it.

Debugging

In order to debug a web page, we can use the Web Development Tools that are available on the browser. On both Google Chrome and Mozilla Firefox, we can bring forward those tools with Ctrl+Shift+i.

We can do many things with the Developer tools:

- we can view the structure of the HTML file and the CSS properties (Elements tab)
- we can see the messages in the console (Console tab)
- we can see the JavaScript code and we can also debug it (Sources tab)
- we can see the network requests and their contents (Network tab)
- and many more

From the Source tab, we can set breakpoints in the JavaScript code. The execution of the code will stop at those points, and then we can see the current values of the variables. We can also run the code step by step, by selecting Step Over (F10). We can also enter inside a function with Step Into (F11). Finally, we can continue with the execution of the code (until the next breakpoint) with Resume Execution (F8).

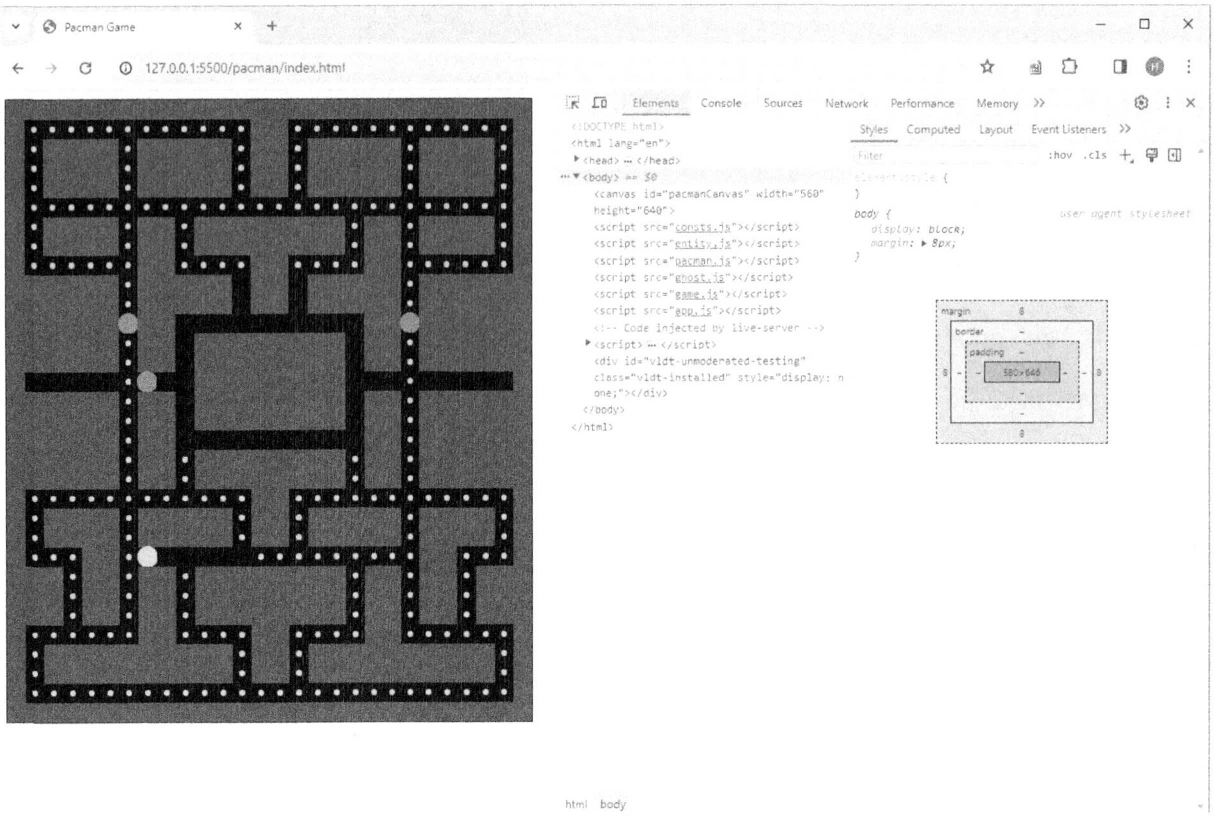
Pacman Game
127.0.0.1:5500/pacman/index.html
Elements
Console
Sources
Network
Performance
Memory
Styles
Computed
Layout
Event Listeners
<html lang="en">
<head> … </head>
<body> == $0
<canvas id="pacmanCanvas" width="560" height="640">
<script src="consts.js"></script>
<script src="entity.js"></script>
<script src="pacman.js"></script>
<script src="ghost.js"></script>
<script src="game.js"></script>
<script src="app.js"></script>
<!-- Code injected by live-server -->
<script> … </script>
<div id="vldt-unmoderated-testing" class="vldt-installed" style="display: none;"></div>
</body>
</html>
body {
display: block;
margin: ▸ 8px;
}
user agent stylesheet
html body

2. Temperature Conversion

For our first project, let's create a simple web application that converts temperatures from Celsius to Fahrenheit degrees and vice versa:

Temperature conversions

Celsius:

Farhenheit:

Convert to Fahrenheit

Convert to Celsius

Concepts covered

- Click event handling
- Number parsing and checking
- CSS styling (Flex)

Proposed Solution

We will begin by creating an HTML file in our folder. In this book, we will follow the convention of naming the main HTML files of the web application as *index.html*.

```
<!DOCTYPE html>
<html>
  <head>
    <title>Temperature conversions</title>
    <link href="style.css" rel="stylesheet">
  </head>
  <body>
    <div class="container">
        <h1>Temperature conversions</h1>
        <label class="item" for="celsius">Celsius:</label>
        <input class="item" type="text" id="celsius"/>
        <label class="item" for="fahrenheit">Farhenheit:</label>
        <input class="item" type="text" id="fahrenheit"/>
        <button type="button" class="item" id="c2f"
          onclick="c2f()">Convert to Fahrenheit</button>
        <button type="button" class="item" id="f2c"
          onclick="f2c()">Convert to Celsius</button>
    </div>
    <script src="script.js" type="text/javascript"></script>
```

```
    </body>
</html>
```

Our application consists of two text boxes (with IDs: `celsius` and `fahrenheit`) and two buttons (with IDs: `c2f` and `f2c`). We will handle the `click` event on both buttons by setting the `onclick` attribute to the corresponding handler function:

```
<button type="button" class="item" id="c2f"
  onclick="c2f()">Convert to Fahrenheit</button>
<button type="button" class="item" id="f2c"
  onclick="f2c()">Convert to Celsius</button>
```

We will implement the two handler functions in a separate JavaScript file (named *script.js*). The JavaScript file will be declared in our HTML file with the following tag:

```
<script src="script.js" type="text/javascript"></script>
```

Now, let's create the *script.js* file in the same folder as the HTML file:

```
function f2c(){
  //get access to the text box elements
  const celsiusEl = document.getElementById("celsius");
  const fahrenheitEl = document.getElementById("fahrenheit");

  //parse text into number
  const fahrenheit = parseFloat(fahrenheitEl.value);

  //check if parsed value is indeed a number
  if(isNaN(fahrenheit)){
    alert("The Fahrenheit value is not correct");
    celsiusEl.value = "";
  }
  else{
    const celsius = (fahrenheit - 32) * 5 / 9;
    //write the result into the celsius text box
    celsiusEl.value = celsius.toFixed(2);
  }
}

function c2f(){
  //get access to the text box elements
  const celsiusEl = document.getElementById("celsius");
  const fahrenheitEl = document.getElementById("fahrenheit");

  //parse text into number
  const celsius = parseFloat(celsiusEl.value);

  //check if parsed value is indeed a number
  if(isNaN(celsius)){
```

```
    alert("The Celsius value is not correct");
    fahrenheitEl.value = "";
  }
  else{
    const fahrenheit = (celsius * 9 / 5) + 32;
    //write the result into the fahrenheit text box
    fahrenheitEl.value = fahrenheit.toFixed(2);
  }
}
```

Both functions operate in a similar manner; first, we obtain the reference to both text input elements (via `getElementById()` function). In this way, we will be able to get access to what the user has typed inside the text boxes, via the `.value` property of each element.

We should note that the `value` property is a `string` value. Therefore, we have to parse the value typed by the user, in order to get the actual numeric value for our calculations. The `parseFloat()` function will start from the beginning of the string value and will parse all numeric characters until a non-numeric character is found. Example conversions:

"1234x" → 1234

"1234x567" → 1234

"x1234" → NaN

The term *NaN* means *Not a Number*; it's a way of specifying that the value is not a number. We can check whether a variable is a number or not with the `isNaN()` function.

In the case where the user has typed a non-numeric string, then an alert will be presented, and the result text box will be left blank. If a numeric string is provided, then we proceed with the calculation, and the result is presented by setting the `value` property of the corresponding text box. The `toFixed(2)` function provides a string representation of the number with two decimal points.

Finally, let's have a look at the CSS file (*style.css*):

```
.container{
  width: 300px;
  /* this is a flex container*/
  display: flex;
  /* items should be placed in a column */
  flex-direction: column;
  /* a gap between items */
  gap: 10px;
}

.item{
  width: 100%;
}
```

```
h1{
  font-size: 1.5em;
}
```

Listing 2-3: style.css

The <div> element that encloses the textboxes and the buttons has the container class assigned to it. This element will become a *flex container*, by setting the display property to flex. We can place the enclosed items in a column with flex-direction: column, and we can also add spacing between them by setting the gap property.

You can find this project in GitHub:

https://github.com/htset/vanilla_javascript_projects/tree/main/temperature1

3. Temperature Conversion (version 2)

Let's refactor the temperature conversion application, so that no buttons are used to initiate the calculations. Instead, the conversions will be performed while the user types a temperature or either type.

Temperature conversions

Celsius:

[   ]

Farhenheit:

[   ]

- Key event handling

In this approach, we only have to change the HTML file:

```
<!DOCTYPE html>
<html>
  <head>
    <title>Temperature conversions</title>
    <link href="style.css" rel="stylesheet">
  </head>
  <body>
    <div class="container">
      <h1>Temperature conversions</h1>
      <label class="item" for="celsius">Celsius:</label>
      <input class="item" type="text"
        id="celsius" onkeyup="c2f()"/>
      <label class="item" for="fahrenheit">Farhenheit:</label>
      <input class="item" type="text"
        id="fahrenheit" onkeyup="f2c()"/>
    </div>
    <script src="script.js" type="text/javascript"></script>
  </body>
</html>
```

Listing 3-1: index.html

In our HTML file, we have removed both buttons that fired the click event for the temperature conversion. Instead, we opt to handle the keyup event, that is fired when we press a key in our keyboard, exactly after we lift our finger from the button. In this way, the conversion result is updated as we are typing the input temperature.

It would be interesting for the reader to experiment with the other two events that are related to typing, keypress and keydown. It turns out that those two events are fired before the actual character is inserted into the text box, so we are always one digit behind from the actual number. Therefore, this makes them unsuitable for our purpose.

The JavaScript and CSS files will remain the same:

```javascript
function f2c(){
  //get access to the text box elements
  const celsiusEl = document.getElementById("celsius");
  const fahrenheitEl = document.getElementById("fahrenheit");

  //parse text into number
  const fahrenheit = parseFloat(fahrenheitEl.value);

  //check if parsed value is indeed a number
  if(isNaN(fahrenheit)){
    alert("The Fahrenheit value is not correct");
    celsiusEl.value = "";
  }
  else{
    const celsius = (fahrenheit - 32) * 5 / 9;
    //write the result into the celsius text box
    celsiusEl.value = celsius.toFixed(2);
  }
}

function c2f(){
  //get access to the text box elements
  const celsiusEl = document.getElementById("celsius");
  const fahrenheitEl = document.getElementById("fahrenheit");

  //parse text into number
  const celsius = parseFloat(celsiusEl.value);

  //check if parsed value is indeed a number
  if(isNaN(celsius)){
    alert("The Celsius value is not correct");
    fahrenheitEl.value = "";
  }
  else{
    const fahrenheit = (celsius * 9 / 5) + 32;
    //write the result into the fahrenheit text box
    fahrenheitEl.value = fahrenheit.toFixed(2);
  }
}
```

Listing 3-2: script.js

```css
.container{
  width: 300px;
  /* this is a flex container*/
  display: flex;
  /* items should be placed in a column */
```

```css
  flex-direction: column;
  /* a gap between items */
  gap: 10px;
}

.item{
  width: 100%;
}

h1{
  font-size: 1.5em;
}
```

Listing 3-3: style.css

You can find this project in GitHub:

https://github.com/htset/vanilla_javascript_projects/tree/main/temperature2

4. Color Picker

We will create a web application that will enable users to play with RGB (Red-Green-Blue) decimal or hex numbers and create colors.

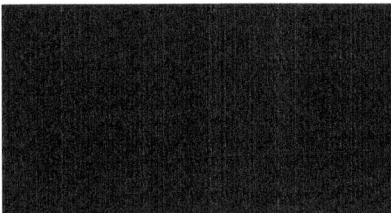

Concepts covered

- Radio box handling
- Setting CSS properties with JavaScript
- Event registration with addEventListener() function

Proposed Solution

First of all, we create our *index.html* file:

```
<!DOCTYPE html>
<html>
  <head>
    <title>Color picker</title>
    <link href="style.css" rel="stylesheet"/>
  </head>
  <body>
    <div class="container">
      <h1>Color picker</h1>
      <div>
        <input type="radio" name="decHex" id="dec" checked/> Decimal
        <input type="radio" name="decHex" id="hex"/> Hex
```

```
      </div>
      <label>Red</label>
      <input type="number" id="red" value="0"/>
      <label>Green</label>
      <input type="number" id="green" value="0"/>
      <label>Blue</label>
      <input type="number" id="blue" value="0"/>
      <div id="panel"></div>
    </div>
    <script src="script.js" type="text/javascript"></script>
  </body>
</html>
```

Listing 4-1: index.html

We use two radio boxes for the selection between decimal and hex values. Note that both radio box elements must have the same name attribute; only then will they be handled as a pair and will be mutually exclusive. If we happen to enter different names, then those radio boxes will be independent from each other, and we will be able to check both of them at the same time!

We also add 3 input elements of type number: this type of element displays up-down buttons for easier number increase and decrease.

Finally, we add a div element that will feature the calculated color in the background.

Note that we do not declare any event handlers in the HTML; we will do it in the following JavaScript file:

```
//get reference to elements
const redEl = document.getElementById("red");
const greenEl = document.getElementById("green");
const blueEl = document.getElementById("blue");
const panelEl = document.getElementById("panel");
const decEl = document.getElementById("dec");
const hexEl = document.getElementById("hex");

//function to calculate color
const calculateColor = function(){
  let red;
  let green;
  let blue;

  if(decEl.checked){
    //if decimal is checked, take value as is
    red = parseInt(redEl.value);
    green = parseInt(greenEl.value);
    blue = parseInt(blueEl.value);
  }
  else{
    //if hex is checked, convert from hex to dec
    red = parseInt(redEl.value, 16);
    green = parseInt(greenEl.value, 16);
```

```javascript
    blue = parseInt(blueEl.value, 16);
  }

  //check for 0-255 range
  if(red < 0 || red > 255 || isNaN(red)
    || green < 0 || green > 255 || isNaN(green)
    || blue < 0 || blue > 255 || isNaN(blue)){

    panelEl.innerHTML = "Values should lie between 0 and 255 (0 and FF)";
    panelEl.style.backgroundColor = "white";
  }
  else{
    panelEl.innerHTML = "";
    //set background color
    panelEl.style.backgroundColor = `rgb(${red}, ${green}, ${blue})`;
  }
}

//change event handler (radio button)
const toggleDecToHex = function(){
  if (decEl.checked){
    redEl.value = parseInt(redEl.value, 16);
    greenEl.value = parseInt(greenEl.value, 16);
    blueEl.value = parseInt(blueEl.value, 16);
  }
  else{
    let tmp = parseInt(redEl.value)
    redEl.value = tmp.toString(16);
    tmp = parseInt(greenEl.value)
    greenEl.value = tmp.toString(16);
    tmp = parseInt(blueEl.value);
    blueEl.value = tmp.toString(16);
  }
}

//register event handlers
redEl.addEventListener("keyup", calculateColor);
greenEl.addEventListener("keyup", calculateColor);
blueEl.addEventListener("keyup", calculateColor);

redEl.addEventListener("change", calculateColor);
greenEl.addEventListener("change", calculateColor);
blueEl.addEventListener("change", calculateColor);

decEl.addEventListener("change", toggleDecToHex);
hexEl.addEventListener("change", toggleDecToHex);

//perform first calculation (all values are 0 by default)
calculateColor();
```

Listing 4-2: script.js

On the top of the JavaScript file, we obtain references to the elements in the HTML. Note that we will follow the convention of adding the suffix "El" to the variable name, so as to make evident that this is an element variable.

Next, we define the color calculation function. Depending on the selected radio button, we either parse the entered value directly (decimal), or we parse it and convert it from hex to decimal (hex).

Then, we check whether all values are within the 0-255 range for RGB numbers. We also check whether the user entered a non-number value. If everything goes well, we set the background color of the div element, by setting the style.backgroundColor property. This is a common example of manipulating CSS properties (in our case, background-color) through JavaScript.

In the case of error input, we revert to white background and display an error message.

Note that we are using Template Literals in order to create the background color string from the color values though string interpolation:

```
panelEl.style.backgroundColor = `rgb(${red}, ${green}, ${blue})`;
```

Next, we define the function that will handle the change event of the radio boxes. We determine the newly selected format value (*dec* or *hex*), and we perform the necessary conversions.

As already mentioned, event handling is defined here, in the JS file. This is performed with the addEventListener() function. This function is called on the specific element object and takes two parameters:

- The name of the event (e.g.: "change")
- The name of the function that will handle the event (e.g. calculateColor)

After registering both types of events (keyup for the text boxes and change for text boxes and radio buttons), we call the calculateColor() function to get the color of the default values (all of them have been defined as 0 in the HTML).

Finally, we should also add a CSS file:

```css
.container{
  width: 300px;
  display: flex;
  flex-direction: column;
  justify-content: center;
  align-items: center;
  gap: 10px;
}

.item{
```

```
  width: 100%;
}

h1{
  font-size: 1.5em;
}

#panel{
  width: 200px;
  height:100px;
  border: 1px black solid;
  text-align: center;
  padding: 5px;
}
```

Listing 4-3: style.css

As in the temperature conversion example, all elements are enclosed inside a flex container and are positioned in a column.

You can find this project in GitHub:

https://github.com/htset/vanilla_javascript_projects/tree/main/color_picker1

5. Color Picker (version 2)

We will continue with the Color Picker web application, and we will replace the text boxes with range controls:

Color picker

◉ Decimal ○ Hex

Red

[slider] 128

Green

[slider] 128

Blue

[slider] 128

Concepts covered

- Slider elements
- State variables

Proposed Solution

First of all, we modify the HTML by adding input elements of type range:

```
<!DOCTYPE html>
<html>
  <head>
    <title>Color picker</title>
    <link href="style.css" rel="stylesheet"/>
  </head>
  <body>
    <div class="container">
      <h1>Color picker</h1>
      <div>
        <input type="radio" name="decHex" id="dec" checked/> Decimal
        <input type="radio" name="decHex" id="hex"/> Hex
      </div>
      <label>Red</label>
```

```html
<div>
  <input type="range" min="0" max="255" id="redRange">
  <input type="text" id="redText"/>
</div>
<label>Green</label>
<div>
  <input type="range" min="0" max="255" id="greenRange">
  <input type="text" id="greenText"/>
</div>
<label>Blue</label>
<div>
  <input type="range" min="0" max="255" id="blueRange">
  <input type="text" id="blueText"/>
</div>
<div id="panel"></div>
  </div>
  <script src="script.js" type="text/javascript"></script>
</body>
</html>
```

Listing 5-1: index.html

The range input element is displayed as a slider in the web browser. We also define *min* and *max* values for the slider range. Next to the slider, we also provide a small text box to display the selected value. Additionally, the text box can be used by the user to enter a value in finer accuracy.

Let's examine the corresponding JavaScript file:

```javascript
//get reference to elements
const redRange = document.getElementById("redRange");
const greenRange = document.getElementById("greenRange");
const blueRange = document.getElementById("blueRange");
const redText = document.getElementById("redText");
const greenText = document.getElementById("greenText");
const blueText = document.getElementById("blueText");
const panelEl = document.getElementById("panel");
const decEl = document.getElementById("dec");
const hexEl = document.getElementById("hex");

//declare and initialize variables
let red = 128;
let green = 128;
let blue = 128;

//function to calculate color from the sliders
const calculateColorFromRange = function(){
  //get values from sliders into the color variables
  red = parseInt(redRange.value);
  green = parseInt(greenRange.value);
  blue = parseInt(blueRange.value);

  //update text boxes
  if(decEl.checked){
```

```
      redText.value = red;
      greenText.value = green;
      blueText.value = blue;
    }
    else{
      redText.value = red.toString(16);
      greenText.value = green.toString(16);
      blueText.value = blue.toString(16);
    }

    if(red < 0 || red > 255 || isNaN(red)
       || green < 0 || green > 255 || isNaN(green)
       || blue < 0 || blue > 255 || isNaN(blue)){

      panelEl.innerHTML = "Values should lie between 0 and 255 (0 and FF)";
      panelEl.style.backgroundColor = "white";
    }
    else{
      panelEl.innerHTML = "";
      panelEl.style.backgroundColor = `rgb(${red}, ${green}, ${blue})`;
    }
}

//function to calculate color from the text boxes
const calculateColorFromText = function(){
  //get values from text boxes into the color variables
  if(decEl.checked){
    red = parseInt(redText.value);
    green = parseInt(greenText.value);
    blue = parseInt(blueText.value);
  }
  else{
    red = parseInt(redText.value, 16);
    green = parseInt(greenText.value, 16);
    blue = parseInt(blueText.value, 16);
  }

  if(red < 0 || red > 255 || isNaN(red)
     || green < 0 || green > 255 || isNaN(green)
     || blue < 0 || blue > 255 || isNaN(blue)){

    panelEl.innerHTML = "Values should lie between 0 and 255 (0 and FF)";
    panelEl.style.backgroundColor = "white";
  }
  else{
    panelEl.innerHTML = "";
    panelEl.style.backgroundColor = `rgb(${red}, ${green}, ${blue})`;
  }

  //update sliders
  redRange.value = red;
  greenRange.value = green;
  blueRange.value = blue;
}
```

```
//change event handler (radio button)
const toggleDecToHex = function(){
  if(decEl.checked){
    redText.value = red;
    greenText.value = green;
    blueText.value = blue;
  }
  else{
    redText.value = red.toString(16);
    greenText.value = green.toString(16);
    blueText.value = blue.toString(16);
  }
}

//register event handlers
redText.addEventListener("keyup", calculateColorFromText);
greenText.addEventListener("keyup", calculateColorFromText);
blueText.addEventListener("keyup", calculateColorFromText);

redRange.addEventListener("change", calculateColorFromRange);
greenRange.addEventListener("change", calculateColorFromRange);
blueRange.addEventListener("change", calculateColorFromRange);

decEl.addEventListener("change", toggleDecToHex);
hexEl.addEventListener("change", toggleDecToHex);

//perform first calculation
calculateColorFromRange();
```

Listing 5-2: script.js

In this version of the Color Picker web app, we have a challenge: there are two types of elements (one slider and one text box) that control the value for each color. In the previous example, we only had one type of element, so we always used the value that was stored in it.

Here, we will define a variable for each color, named red, green and blue. Whenever the user changes the value of an element (e.g. slider), then the color variable will be updated. Moreover, the value of the other element (i.e. text box) will also be updated in order to reflect the new setting.

The three variables can be termed as *state* or *backing* variables, because they are always updated to reflect the *application state*.

After declaring and initializing the three color variables, we proceed with the definition of the two calculating functions (calculateColorFromRange() and calculateColorFromText()). In both functions we perform the following tasks:

- Get the selected value from the element (e.g. redText)
- Update the state variable (e.g. red)

24

- Update the other type of element (e.g. `redRange`)

The CSS file is as follows:

```css
.container{
  width: 300px;
  display: flex;
  flex-direction: column;
  justify-content: center;
  align-items: center;
  gap: 10px;
}

.item{
  width: 100%;
}

h1{
  font-size: 1.5em;
}

#redRange, #blueRange, #greenRange{
  width: 80%;
}

#redText, #blueText, #greenText{
  width: 10%;
}

#panel{
  width: 200px;
  height:100px;
  border: 1px black solid;
  text-align: center;
  padding: 5px;
}
```

Listing 5-3: style.css

You can find this project in GitHub:

https://github.com/htset/vanilla_javascript_projects/tree/main/color_picker2

6. Alarm clock

Here, we will create an alarm clock that will display the current time. By pressing the settings button, the user is presented with the option to set an alarm. The clock will display an alert at the time of the alarm.

Concepts covered

- `setTimeout()` and `setInterval()` functions
- CSS transitions and positioning
- Web fonts
- Date and time handling

Proposed Solution

Let's start with the HTML file:

```
<!DOCTYPE html>
<html>
  <head>
    <title>Digital clock</title>
    <link href="style.css" rel="stylesheet"/>
  </head>
  <body>
    <div id="clock">
      <div id="mainClock">
        <div id="toggleSettings">&#9881;</div>
        <div id="clockDisplay"></div>
      </div>
      <div id="settings" class="fadeOut">
        <div id="timeBox">
            <input type="time" id="alarm">
        </div>
        <div id="buttonBox">
          <button id="setAlarm">Set alarm</button>
          <button id="cancelAlarm">Cancel alarm</button>
        </div>
      </div>
    </div>
    <script src="script.js" type="text/javascript"></script>
  </body>
</html>
```

Listing 6-1: index.html

Our app consists of two main divs, one for the clock (id: mainClock) and one for the settings panel (id: settings). On the clock div, we also have a div (id: toggleSettings) that works as a button and that toggles the visibility of the settings panel. We use the *Gear HTML symbol* whose hex code is ⚙.

On the settings panel, we place an input element of type time; This will make it appear as a time selection element. Finally, there are two buttons for setting and cancelling the alarm.

Let's move to the CSS file:

```
#mainClock{
  width:300px;
  height:150px;
  background-color: darkblue;
  color: white;
  float:left;
  display:flex;
  justify-content: center;
  align-items: center;
  position:relative;
}

#toggleSettings{
  position:absolute;
  bottom:0px;
  right: 0px;
  margin:5px;
  cursor:pointer;
}

#clockDisplay{
  font-size: 3em;
  font-family: alarm;
  width:80%;
  text-align: center;
}

#settings{
  width:300px;
  height:150px;
  background-color:blueviolet;
  color: white;
  float:left;
  opacity:1.0;
  transition: opacity 1s linear;
  display:flex;
  flex-direction: column;
}

#settings.fadeOut{
```

```
  width:300px;
  height:150px;
  background-color:blueviolet;
  color: white;
  float:left;
  display:flex;
  flex-direction: column;
  opacity:0.0;
}

#timeBox, #buttonBox{
  margin: auto;
}

@font-face {
  font-family: alarm;
  src: url(alarm_clock.ttf);
}
```

Listing 6-2: style.css

First of all, we should note that both divs (mainClock and settings) are *floating* to the left of the page, one after the other.

The clock panel uses flexbox to align the clock display vertically and horizontally:

```
display:flex;
justify-content: center;
align-items: center;
```

In order to place the gear image to the bottom right corner of the panel, we use *relative positioning* on the panel and *absolute positioning* on the button:

```
#mainClock{
  position:relative;
}

#toggleSettings{
  position:absolute;
  bottom:0px;
  right: 0px;
}
```

For the clock display (id: clockDisplay) we use a web font that resembles that of a real digital clock. We will have to download it from the following link:

https://www.dafont.com/alarm-clock.font

We should place the font file (*alarm_clock.ttf*) in the project folder and reference it in the CSS file:

```css
@font-face {
  font-family: alarm;
  src: url(alarm_clock.ttf);
}

#clockDisplay{
  font-family: alarm;
}
```

Let's move on to the settings panel. This panel is hidden on page load and is displayed when the settings button is pressed. We will create a CSS class (.fadeOut) that will be applied when the panel is hidden:

```css
#settings{
  opacity:1.0;
  transition: opacity 1s linear;
}

#settings.fadeOut{
  opacity:0.0;
  transition: opacity 2s linear;
}
```

The effect of hiding and displaying the panel is achieved with the use of the opacity property that takes values between 0 and 1. We also use the transition property to make the change in opacity smoother. Note that for example's sake we use different transition durations (1 sec and 2 sec) when the panel is displayed and hidden respectively.

Now, it's time to move on the JavaScript file:

```javascript
const toggleSettingsEl = document.getElementById("toggleSettings");
const setAlarmEl = document.getElementById("setAlarm");
const cancelAlarmEl = document.getElementById("cancelAlarm");
const clockEl = document.getElementById("clockDisplay");
const settingsEl = document.getElementById("settings");

const timeHandler = function (){
  let currentTime = new Date();
  let hours = currentTime.getHours() < 10?
    "0"+currentTime.getHours() : currentTime.getHours();
  let minutes = currentTime.getMinutes() < 10?
    "0" + currentTime.getMinutes() : currentTime.getMinutes();
  let seconds = currentTime.getSeconds() < 10?
    "0" + currentTime.getSeconds() : currentTime.getSeconds();
  clockEl.innerHTML = `${hours}:${minutes}:${seconds}`;
}

const toggleSettings = function(){
  if (settingsEl.classList.contains("fadeOut")) {
```

```javascript
      settingsEl.classList.remove("fadeOut");
  }
  else {
    settingsEl.classList.add("fadeOut");
  }
}

const setAlarm = function(){
  if(document.getElementById("alarm").value != ''){
    let currentTime = new Date();
    let selectedTime = document.getElementById("alarm").value.split(":");
    let alarmTime;
    if(selectedTime[0] < currentTime.getHours()
      || (selectedTime[0] == currentTime.getHours()
         && selectedTime[1] < currentTime.getMinutes()))
      alarmTime = new Date(currentTime.getFullYear(),
                           currentTime.getMonth(),
                           currentTime.getDate()+1,
                           selectedTime[0],
                           selectedTime[1],
                           0);
    else
      alarmTime = new Date(currentTime.getFullYear(),
                           currentTime.getMonth(),
                           currentTime.getDate(),
                           selectedTime[0],
                           selectedTime[1],
                           0);

    let duration = alarmTime.getTime() - currentTime.getTime();
    clearTimeout(alarm);
    alarm = setTimeout(alarmHandler, duration);
  }
}

const cancelAlarm = function(){
  clearTimeout(alarm);
  let alarmTime = document.getElementById("alarm").value = '';
}

const alarmHandler = function(){
  alert("Rrrrriinggggg!");
}

toggleSettingsEl.addEventListener("click", toggleSettings);
setAlarmEl.addEventListener("click", setAlarm);
cancelAlarmEl.addEventListener("click", cancelAlarm);

let alarm = '';
let timer = setInterval(timeHandler, 1000);
```

Listing 6-3: script.js

The current time is displayed on the clock display with the use of the `setInterval()` function.This function is run once at the end of the file and, as a result, it calls the `timeHandler()` function every second. The `timeHandler()` function gets the current time and breaks it into hours, minutes and seconds, and prints them using a template string.

The `toggleSettings()` function hides or shows the settings panel, by adding or removing the `fadeOut` class respectively.

In the `setAlarm()` function, we first get the current date and time. Then we create a new `Date` object based on the alarm time and we subtract their total time values that we get with the `Date.getTime()` function. We use the duration (in milliseconds) to set an alarm with `setTimeout()`: when the timeout is complete, the callback function `alarmHandler()` will be called and will show the `alert()` message box. Note that we are also clearing any existing alarms with `clearTimeout()`, before setting a new alarm.

You can find this project in GitHub:

https://github.com/htset/vanilla_javascript_projects/tree/main/clock

7. Todo List

Let's create a todo list, where the tasks typed by the user are entered in a dynamic list. Users will also be able to delete a todo from the list.

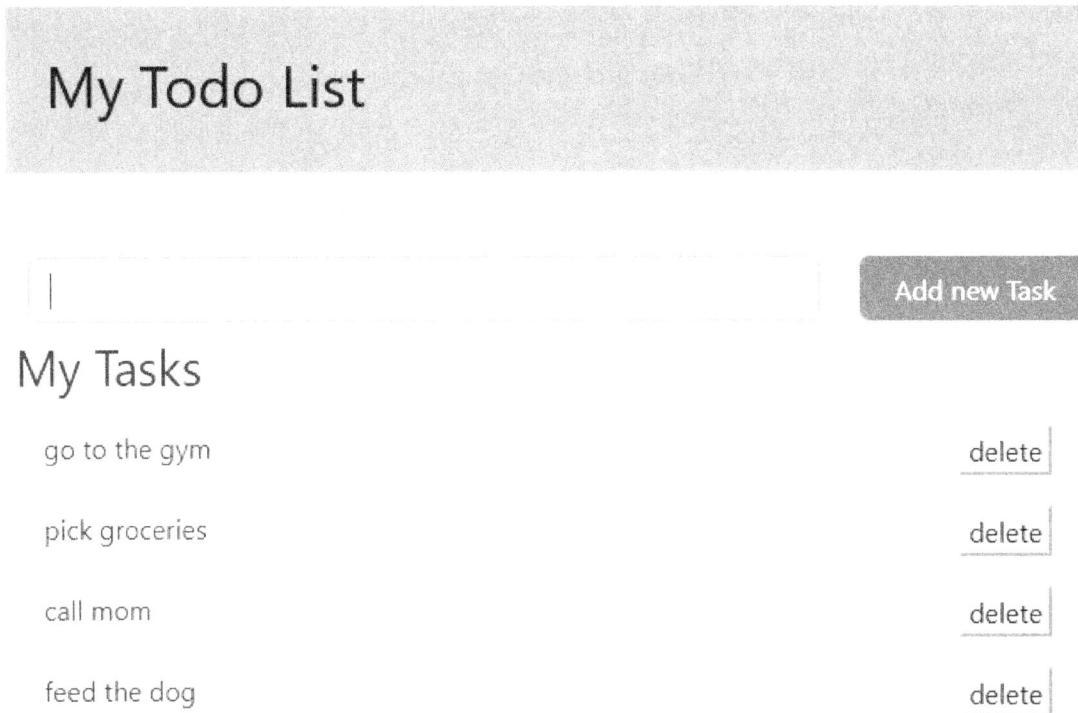

My Todo List

	Add new Task

My Tasks

go to the gym	delete
pick groceries	delete
call mom	delete
feed the dog	delete

Concepts covered

- Bootstrap use
- Adding and removing DOM elements
- Arrow functions
- Form handling

Proposed Solution

As always, we will start with the HTML file:

```
<!DOCTYPE html>
<html lang="en">
<head>
  <link
href="https://cdn.jsdelivr.net/npm/bootstrap@5.2.3/dist/css/bootstrap.min.css"
rel="stylesheet"
integrity="sha384-rbsA2VBKQhggwzxH7pPCaAqO46MgnOM80zW1RWuH61DGLwZJEdK2Kadq2F9CUG65"
crossorigin="anonymous">
</head>
<body>
```

```
<div class="container">
  <header class="bg-info text-black p-4 m-4">
      <h1>My Todo List</h1>
  </header>

  <div class="container">
    <div class="card card-body">
      <form action="" id="form">
        <div class="row">
          <div class="col-md-9">
            <input type="text" class="form-control m-2" id="text">
          </div>
          <div class="col-md-3">
            <input type="submit" class="form-control btn btn-success m-2"
              value="Add new Task">
          </div>
        </div>
      </form>
      <h2 class="title">My Tasks</h2>
      <ul id="items" class="list-group">

      </ul>
    </div>
  </div>
</div>
<script
src="https://cdn.jsdelivr.net/npm/bootstrap@5.2.3/dist/js/bootstrap.bundle.min.js"
integrity="sha384-kenU1KFdBIe4zVF0s0G1M5b4hcpxyD9F7jL+jjXkk+Q2h455rYXK/7HAuoJl+0I4"
crossorigin="anonymous"></script>
  <script src="script.js" type="text/javascript"></script>
</body>
</html>
```

Listing 7-1: index.html

In order to get a nice aesthetic result, we will be using the *Bootstrap library* in some of our projects. Boostrap can be enabled by importing a CSS and a JavaScript file in the HTML, using the <link> and <script> tags respectively.

Note that, in the above listing, we choose to load the library from a Content Delivery Network (CDN). This means that when the user loads the web page, the browser will download the two files from the CDN. As an alternative, we can download those files and make them available through our own web server (we should not forget to update their links in the HTML). Bootstrap 5.2.3 was the latest version at the time of writing this book.

The user interface consists of a form element with an input box and a submit button. When the user presses the submit button, the form is not sent to the server (since the form action attribute is empty). Instead, the typed text will be entered in an unordered list below.

All elements are enclosed in a container div. This web application does not contain any CSS files; styling is performed by applying Bootstrap classes on the elements. For instance, the <header> element has the following classes:

```
<header class="bg-info text-black p-4 m-4">
```

The applied classes define the following styling:

- background: "info" (light blue)
- text: black
- padding: size 4
- margin: size 4

Now, let's examine the JS file:

```
const formEl = document.getElementById("form");
const itemsEl = document.getElementById("items");
const textEl = document.getElementById("text");

const handleSubmit = (e) => {
  //create new <li> element
  const item = document.createElement("li");
  //add TextNode inside <li>
  const textnode = document.createTextNode(textEl.value);
  item.appendChild(textnode);

  //set element attributes
  item.setAttribute("class", "list-group-item");
  item.setAttribute("name", "list");

  //add Delete button to <li>
  const button = document.createElement("button");
  button.innerHTML = "delete";
  button.style.float = "right";
  button.addEventListener("click", deleteTodo);
  item.appendChild(button);

  //add <li> to <ul> list
  itemsEl.appendChild(item);

  //empty text box
  textEl.value = '';

  //prevent form submission
  e.preventDefault();
}

const deleteTodo = (e) => {
  //find the parent element of the button (--> the <li> element)
  //and remove it from the DOM
  e.target.parentElement.remove();
```

```
}
//attach event listener
formEl.addEventListener("submit", handleSubmit);
```

Listing 7-2: script.js

As we see at the bottom of the file, when using forms, we should handle the submit event. Therefore, when the user presses the submit button, or presses the *Enter button* at the keyboard, then function handleSubmit() is called.

Here, we use a different way to declare a function, by using an *arrow function*. We can use the following form:

```
const functionName = (arg1, arg2, ..) => { ...   };
```

which is equivalent to this:

```
const functionName = function(arg1, arg2, ..) { ...   };
```

and this:

```
function functionName(arg1, arg2, ..) { ...   };
```

In handleSubmit() we first create a new list element (<li>) by using the document.createElement() function. Afterwards, we create a TextNode that will represent the internal of the list element. We then append it in the list element.

Next, we apply two attributes on the list element: we set the class and the name of the element.

Furthermore, we create a button element, that will serve as the delete button. We set the innerHTML value to the text that should appear on the button and we set the style of the button as "float:right".

When the delete button is pressed, the deleteTodo() function should be invoked. This is performed by adding an event listener on this element.

Then, we append the button in the list element, and we also append the resulting list element into the unordered list.

Finally, we call function preventDefault() on the submit event that was triggered; this will prevent the form from submitting to the server, in case the action attribute was set.

Now, let's have a look at the deleteTodo() function. In this one-liner, we first get the element that triggered the event (e.target) – i.e. the delete button – then we get its parent (`e.target.parent`) – i.e. the list element – and then we remove the parent from its container – i.e. the list.

You can find this project in GitHub:

https://github.com/htset/vanilla_javascript_projects/tree/main/todo1

8. Todo List (version 2)

We will enhance the Todo List application of the previous project, so that users will be able to rearrange the items in the list using drag and drop.

Concepts covered

- Drag and drop
- DOM manipulation

Proposed Solution

The *index.html* file will remain unchanged:

```
<!DOCTYPE html>
<html lang="en">
<head>
  <link
    href="https://cdn.jsdelivr.net/npm/bootstrap@5.2.3/dist/css/bootstrap.min.css"
    rel="stylesheet"
    integrity="sha384-
rbsA2VBKQhggwzxH7pPCaAqO46MgnOM80zW1RWuH61DGLwZJEdK2Kadq2F9CUG65"
    crossorigin="anonymous">
</head>
<body>
  <div class="container">
    <header class="bg-info text-black p-4 m-4">
        <h1>My Todo List</h1>
    </header>

    <div class="container">
      <div class="card card-body">
        <form action="" id="form">
          <div class="row">
            <div class="col-md-9">
              <input type="text" class="form-control m-2" id="text">
            </div>
            <div class="col-md-3">
              <input type="submit" class="form-control btn btn-success m-2"
                value="Add new Task">
            </div>
          </div>
        </form>
        <h2 class="title">My Tasks</h2>
        <ul id="items" class="list-group">

        </ul>
      </div>
    </div>
  </div>
  <script
src="https://cdn.jsdelivr.net/npm/bootstrap@5.2.3/dist/js/bootstrap.bundle.min.js"
integrity="sha384-kenU1KFdBIe4zVF0s0G1M5b4hcpxyD9F7jL+jjXkk+Q2h455rYXK/7HAuoJl+0I4"
```

```
    crossorigin="anonymous"></script>
  <script src="script.js" type="text/javascript"></script>
</body>
</html>
```

We will have to update the JavaScript file in order to provide drag and drop functionality to the user:

```javascript
const formEl = document.getElementById("form");
const itemsEl = document.getElementById("items");
const textEl = document.getElementById("text");

let draggedItem;

const handleSubmit = (e) => {
  //create new <li> element
  const item = document.createElement("li");
  //add TextNode inside <li>
  const textnode = document.createTextNode(textEl.value);
  item.appendChild(textnode);

  //set element attributes
  item.setAttribute("class", "list-group-item");
  item.setAttribute("name", "list");
  item.setAttribute("draggable", "true");

  //add Delete button to <li>
  const button = document.createElement("button");
  button.innerHTML = "delete";
  button.style.float = "right";
  button.addEventListener("click", deleteTodo);
  item.appendChild(button);

  //add <li> to <ul> list
  itemsEl.appendChild(item);

  //empty text box
  textEl.value = '';

  //prevent form submission
  e.preventDefault();
}

const deleteTodo = (e) => {
  //find the parent element of the button (--> the <li> element)
  //and remove it from the DOM
  e.target.parentElement.remove();
}

//called when dragging starts
const handleDragStart = (e) => {
  draggedItem = e.target;
```

```
    e.dataTransfer.effectAllowed = 'move';
    e.dataTransfer.setData('text/html', draggedItem.innerHTML);
}

//called when the item is dragged over another item
const handleDragOver = (e) => {
  e.preventDefault();
}

//called when the item is dropped
const handleDrop = (e) => {
  e.preventDefault();
  //check whether it will be placed before or after the target element
  if(e.target !== draggedItem && e.target.classList.contains('list-group-item')) {
    if(e.clientY>e.target.getBoundingClientRect().top+(e.target.offsetHeight / 2)) {
      //drop it after the item --> i.e. before the next sibling of the item
      e.target.parentNode.insertBefore(draggedItem, e.target.nextSibling);
    }
    else {
      //drop it before the item
      e.target.parentNode.insertBefore(draggedItem, e.target);
    }
  }
  draggedItem = null;
}

//attach event listeners
itemsEl.addEventListener("dragstart", handleDragStart);
itemsEl.addEventListener("dragover", handleDragOver);
itemsEl.addEventListener("drop", handleDrop);
formEl.addEventListener("submit",handleSubmit);
```

Listing 8-2: script.js

First of all, we should mark list items as *draggable*. For this, we add the draggable attribute
when we create a new list item:

```
item.setAttribute("draggable", "true");
```

Furthermore, in addition to the submit event, we will have to handle the following events:

- dragstart: fired when dragging starts
- dragover: fired when the dragged item is over the target item
- drop: fired when the dragged item is dropped on the target item

We will add event listeners for these three events by calling addEventListener() on the
items list element. We define three event handlers:

```
handleDragStart()
handleDragOver()
handleDrop()
```

41

When dragging starts, we keep the reference to the dragged item (e.target) in a variable; it will be needed in the other functions.

The event object (e) contains a dataTransfer object. With the dataTransfer object we can specify the effect that will take place (in our case, move the item to another place). We also specify that we are going to move HTML (i.e., the innerHTML value of the item).

When the item is moved over the list (which is a valid drop target), then the dragover event is fired. In the handler function we call e.preventDefault(), which enables it to receive drop events.

Finally, when the item is dropped inside the list, we first prevent the default handling of the item (the default behaviour is to open as link on drop). The argument of the handler function handleDrop(e) is the actual event fired. From this event we can get the target element, i.e. the element on which the dragged item was dropped.

First, we make sure that the target element is not the dragged element itself (this will happen when the dragged element has not been moved) and that the target element is of the list-group-item class (i.e. it is a list item). Then, we do some measuring, in order to find out whether we will insert the dragged item before or after the aforementioned list item.

Depending on whether we dropped it on the top or the bottom half of the list item, the dragged item will be inserted (with insertBefore()) before the item itself or the next sibling of the item respectively.

You can find this project in GitHub:

https://github.com/htset/vanilla_javascript_projects/tree/main/todo2

9. Todo List (version 3)

In the third part of the Todo List saga, we will again refactor our application, by keeping the application state (the todo entries) into an array. Moreover, the todo entries will be stored in localStorage, in order to be available between application reloads.

Concepts covered

- JS array manipulation
- Local storage

Proposed Solution

The application that we created in the previous chapter works pretty well. However, it still has some shortcomings. For instance, when the web page reloads, the tasks are lost, and we have to enter them all over again. For this reason, we will use *localStorage* in order to store the todo entries into the browser's storage space and have them available, even when our web page reloads.

Furthermore, the application maintains our data (i.e. the todo entries) inside the HTML, since the entries text is entered inside list item (`<li>`) elements. This is not very efficient; for instance, if we wanted to get the text of a specific todo entry, then we would have to use DOM manipulation and get the `innerHTML` value of the respective list item.

Given that we also need to store the todo entries into localStorage, it would be better to maintain all the entries in an array of strings. Whenever the user adds, deletes or drags a todo entry, then this array will be updated, and the modified array will be used to re-render the todo list in the web page.

The HTML code of our project will remain unchanged:

```
<!DOCTYPE html>
<html lang="en">
<head>
  <link
href="https://cdn.jsdelivr.net/npm/bootstrap@5.2.3/dist/css/bootstrap.min.css"
  rel="stylesheet"                                    integrity="sha384-
rbsA2VBKQhggwzxH7pPCaAqO46MgnOM80zW1RWuH61DGLwZJEdK2Kadq2F9CUG65"
  crossorigin="anonymous">
</head>
<body>
  <div class="container">
    <header class="bg-info text-black p-4 m-4">
        <h1>My Todo List</h1>
    </header>

    <div class="container">
      <div class="card card-body">
        <form action="" id="form">
          <div class="row">
```

```html
        <div class="col-md-9">
          <input type="text" class="form-control m-2" id="text">
        </div>
        <div class="col-md-3">
          <input type="submit" class="form-control btn btn-success m-2"
            value="Add new Task">
        </div>
      </div>
    </form>
    <h2 class="title">My Tasks</h2>
    <ul id="items" class="list-group">

    </ul>
      </div>
    </div>
  </div>
  <script
  src="https://cdn.jsdelivr.net/npm/bootstrap@5.2.3/dist/js/bootstrap.bundle.min.js"
  integrity="sha384-kenU1KFdBIe4zVF0s0G1M5b4hcpxyD9F7jL+jjXkk+Q2h455rYXK/7HAuoJl+0I4"
  crossorigin="anonymous"></script>
  <script src="script.js" type="text/javascript"></script>
</body>
</html>
```

Listing 9-1: index.html

We will have to refactor the JavaScript code:

```javascript
const formEl = document.getElementById("form");
const itemsEl = document.getElementById("items");
const textEl = document.getElementById("text");

let draggedItem, draggedItemID;

//re-create unordered list based on the array of tasks
const renderList = () => {
  //first delete the existing entries
  itemsEl.innerHTML = '';

  for (let id in tasks) {
    //create new <li> element
    const item = document.createElement("li");
    //add TextNode inside <li>
    const textnode = document.createTextNode(tasks[id]);
    item.appendChild(textnode);

    //set element attributes
    item.setAttribute("class", "list-group-item");
    item.setAttribute("name", "list");
    item.setAttribute("draggable", "true");
    item.setAttribute("data-id", id); //custom attribute

    //add Delete button to <li>
    let button = document.createElement("button");
    button.innerHTML = "delete";
```

44

```
      button.style.float = "right";
      button.addEventListener("click", deleteTodo);
      item.appendChild(button);

      //add <li> to <ul> list
      itemsEl.appendChild(item);
  }
}

const deleteTodo = (e) => {
  //get the index of the element via the data-id custom attribute
  const targetID = e.target.parentNode.getAttribute("data-id");
  //remove task from array
  tasks.splice(targetID, 1);
  renderList();
  //replace modified array in local storage
  localStorage.setItem("tasks", JSON.stringify(tasks));
}

//called when dragging starts
const handleDragStart = (e) => {
  draggedItem = e.target;
  //keep the id of the moved item in a variable
  draggedItemID = e.target.getAttribute("data-id");
  e.dataTransfer.effectAllowed = 'move';
  e.dataTransfer.setData('text/html', draggedItem.innerHTML);
}

//called when the item is dragged over another item
const handleDragOver = (e) => {
  e.preventDefault();
}

//called when the item is dropped
const handleDrop = (e) => {
  e.preventDefault();
  //check whether it will be placed before or after the target element
  if (e.target !== draggedItem && e.target.classList.contains('list-group-item')) {
    //get the id of the list item over which the dragged item was dropped
    let targetId = parseInt(e.target.getAttribute("data-id"));
    //removed the dragged item id from the array
    let taskText = tasks.splice(draggedItemID, 1);

    if (e.clientY>e.target.getBoundingClientRect().top+(e.target.offsetHeight / 2)) {
      if (targetId < draggedItemID) {
        //create new tasks array while inserting the dragged item
        tasks = [
          ...tasks.slice(0, targetId + 1),
          taskText[0],
          ...tasks.slice(targetId + 1)
        ];
      }
      else {
        tasks = [
```

```
          ...tasks.slice(0, targetId),
          taskText[0],
          ...tasks.slice(targetId)
        ];
      }
    }
    else {
      if (targetId < draggedItemID) {
        tasks = [
          ...tasks.slice(0, targetId),
          taskText[0],
          ...tasks.slice(targetId)
        ];
      }
      else {
        tasks = [
          ...tasks.slice(0, targetId - 1),
          taskText[0],
          ...tasks.slice(targetId - 1)
        ];
      }
    }
  }
  renderList();
  //replace modified array in local storage
  localStorage.setItem("tasks", JSON.stringify(tasks));
  draggedItem = null;
}

const handleSubmit = (e) => {
  e.preventDefault();
  //insert task text into array
  tasks.push(text.value);
  renderList();
  //replace modified array in local storage
  localStorage.setItem("tasks", JSON.stringify(tasks));
  //empty text box
  text.value = '';
}

//attach event listeners
itemsEl.addEventListener("dragstart", handleDragStart);
itemsEl.addEventListener("dragover", handleDragOver);
itemsEl.addEventListener("drop", handleDrop);
formEl.addEventListener("submit", handleSubmit);

//startup
let tasks = JSON.parse(localStorage.getItem("tasks"));
if (tasks == undefined)
  tasks = [];
else
  renderList();
```

Listing 9-2: script.js

First of all, we should mention that we are using a JS array called `tasks` to store the todo strings. Let's break down the code into the various functions:

renderList

The `renderList()` function iterates over the `tasks` array and builds the unordered list. The code is almost the same from the previous versions. However, note that we apply a custom attribute (called `data-id`) on each list item element. This attribute will store the index number of the item inside the `tasks` list.

deleteTodo

This function is called when the delete button is clicked. Instead of performing DOM manipulation by removing the list item element, it removes the respective string from the `tasks` array, using `splice()`. Next, the todo list is rendered all over again, using the newly modified `tasks` array.

Finally, the modified `tasks` array is stored in localStorage. To achieve this, we use the `JSON.stringify()` function in order to get a string representation of the JS array in JSON.

handleDragStart

When drag and drop starts, we also keep the ID of the dragged item. We get this ID from the `data-id` custom attribute of the list element.

handleDragOver

This function remains unchanged.

handleDrop

When the user drops the item in a new place in the list, then we first get the ID of the list element over which the dragged item was dropped. Then, we delete the dragged item from the `tasks` array.

Next, we create a new `tasks` array (in place of the existing one) by using the *spread operator* (...). There are various cases, depending on where the dragged item was dropped (i.e. on the upper or lower half of the list item).

Finally, we re-render the todo list by calling `render()` and we store the modified array in the localStorage.

handleSubmit

The `handleSubmit()` function pushes the new todo text into the `tasks` array and calls `render()`. It also empties the text box.

Apart from the functions, we add the necessary event listeners, and at the startup of the application, we check the localStorage for the existence of a todo list. If so, we parse the stored JSON string and we assign it to the tasks array. In the absence of any list, the `tasks` variable is initialized as an empty array. Finally, `render()` is called for the first time to create the unordered list in the HTML.

You can find this project in GitHub:

https://github.com/htset/vanilla_javascript_projects/tree/main/todo3

10. Form validation

In this project, we will create an extensive registration form and we will perform client-side validation using JavaScript.

Registration Form

First name

Last name

Gender
Male Female N/A

Zip code

State
New York ∨

Address

Email:

Telephone:

☐ I have read and agree to the terms of service
☐ I agree to receive information

Comments

Select password:

Confirm password:

Submit

The form contents should follow the following rules:

- All data should be entered, with the exception of the Address field. However, if the state entered is *Colorado*, then the address should be filled in as well.
- The ZIP code should consist of 5 numbers only
- The user should enter a valid email (xxx@xxx.xx)
- The phone number should be in the form of (123)456-7890, 1234567890 or 123-456-7890
- The user should at least accept the terms of service

When the submit button is pressed, the validation results will be printed, with red color, next to the respective element.

Concepts covered

- Form handling and validation

Proposed Solution

Let's start with the *index.html* file:

```html
<!DOCTYPE html>
<html lang="en">

<head>
  <title>Registration sample</title>
  <meta http-equiv="Content-Type" content="text/html; charset=utf-8">
  <link
href="https://cdn.jsdelivr.net/npm/bootstrap@5.2.3/dist/css/bootstrap.min.css"
rel="stylesheet"
    integrity="sha384-
rbsA2VBKQhggwzxH7pPCaAqO46MgnOM80zW1RWuH61DGLwZJEdK2Kadq2F9CUG65"
crossorigin="anonymous">
  <link href="style.css" rel="stylesheet" />
</head>

<body>
  <h3>Registration Form</h3>
  <form onsubmit="return validate();">

    <label for="fname">First name</label><br />
    <input type="text" name="fname" id="fname" />
    <span id="fnameError" class="error"></span><br />

    <label for="lname">Last name</label><br />
    <input type="text" name="lname" id="lname" />
    <span id="lnameError" class="error"></span><br /><br />

    <label>Gender</label><br />
    <input type="radio" value="Male" name="gender" id="male" />
    <label for="male">Male</label>
    <input type="radio" value="Female" name="gender" id="female" />
```

```
<label for="female">Female</label>
<input type="radio" value="NA" name="gender" id="na" />
<label for="na">N/A</label>
<span id="genderError" class="error"></span><br /><br />

<label for="zip">Zip code</label><br />
<input type="text" name="zip" id="zip" />
<span id="zipError" class="error"></span><br />

<label for="state">State</label><br />
<select id="state" name="state">
  <option value="NY">New York</option>
  <option value="CA">California</option>
  <option value="CO">Colorado</option>
  <option value="TX">Texas</option>
</select><span id="stateError" class="error"></span><br /><br />

<label for="address">Address</label><br />
<input type="text" name="address" id="address" />
<span id="addressError" class="error"></span><br />

<label for="email">Email:</label><br />
<input type="text" name="email" id="email" />
<span id="emailError" class="error"></span><br />

<label for="phone">Telephone:</label><br />
<input type="text" name="phone" id="phone" />
<span id="phoneError" class="error"></span><br /><br />

<input type="checkbox" value="accept" name="checks" id="accept">
<label for="accept">I have read and agree to the terms of service</label>
<span id="acceptError" class="error"></span><br />

<input type="checkbox" value="inform" name="checks" id="inform">
<label for="inform">I agree to receive information</label>
<span id="informError" class="error"></span><br /><br />

<label for="comments">Comments</label><br />
<textarea rows="5" cols="40" name="comments" id="comments"
  wrap="physical"></textarea><br /><br />

<label for="password">Select password:</label><br />
<input type="password" name="password" id="password" />
<span id="passwordError" class="error"></span><br />

<label for="confirm">Confirm password:</label><br />
<input type="password" name="confirm" id="confirm" />
<span id="confirmError" class="error"></span><br /><br />

<input type="submit" value="Submit" /><br />

</form>
<script
src="https://cdn.jsdelivr.net/npm/bootstrap@5.2.3/dist/js/bootstrap.bundle.min.js"
```

```
    integrity="sha384-
kenU1KFdBIe4zVF0s0G1M5b4hcpxyD9F7jL+jjXkk+Q2h455rYXK/7HAuoJl+0I4"
    crossorigin="anonymous"></script>
  <script src="script.js" type="text/javascript"></script>
</body>

</html>
```
Listing 10-1: index.html

Our registration form contains a variety of elements:

- Text boxes
- Password text boxes
- Check boxes
- Radio boxes
- Drop-down list
- Text area
- Submit button

Moreover, next to each element there is a `<span>` element that will contain the respective error message. We apply the `error` class to these elements.

Apart from that, the HTML is pretty straightforward, so we will proceed to the JavaScript file:

```
const fname = document.getElementById("fname");
const lname = document.getElementById("lname");
const gender = document.getElementsByName("gender");
const zip = document.getElementById("zip");
const state = document.getElementById("state");
const address = document.getElementById("address");
const email = document.getElementById("email");
const phone = document.getElementById("phone");
const checks = document.getElementsByName("checks");
const password = document.getElementById("password");
const confirm = document.getElementById("confirm");
const comments = document.getElementById("comments");

const fnameError = document.getElementById("fnameError");
const lnameError = document.getElementById("lnameError");
const genderError = document.getElementsByName("genderError");
const zipError = document.getElementById("zipError");
const stateError = document.getElementById("stateError");
const addressError = document.getElementById("addressError");
const emailError = document.getElementById("emailError");
const phoneError = document.getElementById("phoneError");
const checksError = document.getElementsByName("checksError");
const passwordError = document.getElementById("passwordError");
const confirmError = document.getElementById("confirmError");

const errorSpans = document.getElementsByClassName("error");
```

```javascript
const validate = function() {
  let result = true;

  //remove previous errors
  for(let i=0; i<errorSpans.length; i++){
    errorSpans[i].innerHTML = "";
  }

  if(fname.value == ""){
    fnameError.innerHTML = "First name is required";
    result = false;
  }

  if(lname.value == ""){
    lnameError.innerHTML = "Last name is required";
    result = false;
  }

  let found = false;
  for (let i = 0; i < gender.length; i++) {
    if (gender[i].checked === true)
      found = true;
  }
  if(!found){
    genderError.innerHTML = "Gender is required";
    result = false;
  }

  if (zip.value == "") {
    zipError.innerHTML = "ZIP is required";
    result = false;
  }
  else if (zip.value.length != 5 || isNaN(zip.value)) {
    zipError.innerHTML = "ZIP is not correct";
    result = false;
  }

  if (state.value === "CO") {
    if(address.value == ""){
      addressError.innerHTML = "Address is required for Colorado";
      result = false;
    }
  }

  const                    emailRegex                    =
/^(([^<>()[\]\\.,;:\s@"]+(\.[^<>()[\]\\.,;:\s@"]+)*)|.(".+"))@((\[[0-9]{1,3}\.[0-
9]{1,3}\.[0-9]{1,3}\.[0-9]{1,3}\])|(([a-zA-Z\-0-9]+\.)+[a-zA-Z]{2,}))$/;
  if (!email.value.match(emailRegex)){
    emailError.innerHTML = "Email is not correct";
    result = false;
  }

  const phoneRegex = /^\(?(\d{3})\)?[- ]?(\d{3})[- ]?(\d{4})$/;
  if (!phone.value.match(phoneRegex)){
```

```
      phoneError.innerHTML  =  "Phone  formats:  (123)456-7890,  1234567890  or  123-456-
7890";
    result = false;
  }

  if(checks[0].checked === false){
    acceptError.innerHTML = "You should agree to the terms";
    result = false;
  }

  if(password.value.length < 8){
    passwordError.innerHTML = "Password should contain at least 8 characters";
    result = false;
  }
  if(confirm.value !== password.value){
    confirmError.innerHTML = "Password and Confirm Password do not match";
    result = false;
  }

  return result;
}
```

Listing 10-2: script.js

At the start of the file, we get the references to all the elements in the HTML file. We also get an array of all the error elements, which we will use to loop through and empty the previous error messages:

```
const errorSpans = document.getElementsByClassName("error");
```

The only function is `validate()`; it is called when the user presses the submit button. Note the form definition in the HTML file:

```
<form onsubmit="return validate();">
```

We use this syntax so that we can prevent the submission of the form, if the `validate()` function returns false.

First of all, we empty the error spans from the previous validation, if any:

```
  for(let i=0; i<errorSpans.length; i++){
    errorSpans[i].innerHTML = "";
  }
```

Then, we check whether the text element for the first name is empty:

```
  if(fname.value == ""){
    fnameError.innerHTML = "First name is required";
    result = false;
  }
```

Note the use of the `result` variable. At first it is true, and if any validation fails, then it is turned into false. At the end of the validation function we will eventually return the value of this variable. The same value check is performed for the last name and address text boxes.

In order to check whether a radio box is checked, we have to get all the radio boxes using their `name` property:

```
const gender = document.getElementsByName("gender");
```

The `gender` object is an element array that contains all the radio boxes under the name "gender". We then loop over this array in an effort to find one element whose `checked` property is true:

```
let found = false;
for (let i = 0; i < gender.length; i++) {
  if (gender[i].checked === true)
    found = true;
}
if(!found){
  genderError.innerHTML = "Gender is required";
  result = false;
}
```

Next, we check whether the ZIP value is not empty and that it is a string of 5 digits only:

```
if (zip.value == "") {
  zipError.innerHTML = "ZIP is required";
  result = false;
}
else if (zip.value.length != 5 || isNaN(zip.value)) {
  zipError.innerHTML = "ZIP is not correct";
  result = false;
}
```

We use the `isNaN()` function to test whether the string contains only numbers or not.

Then, we check the state value; if the selected state is Colorado (id=="CO"), then the user should also fill in the address field:

```
if (state.value === "CO") {
  if(address.value == ""){
    addressError.innerHTML = "Address is required for Colorado";
    result = false;
  }
}
```

For the email and phone validation we will use regular expressions (regex):

```
const                              emailRegex                              =
/^(([^<>()[\]\\.,;:\s@"]+(\.[^<>()[\]\\.,;:\s@"]+)*)|.(".+"))@((\[[0-9]{1,3}\.[0-
9]{1,3}\.[0-9]{1,3}\.[0-9]{1,3}\])|(([a-zA-Z\-0-9]+\.)+[a-zA-Z]{2,}))$/;
  if (!email.value.match(emailRegex)){
    emailError.innerHTML = "Email is not correct";
    result = false;
  }

  const phoneRegex = /^\(?(\d{3})\)?[- ]?(\d{3})[- ]?(\d{4})$/;
  if (!phone.value.match(phoneRegex)){
    phoneError.innerHTML = "Phone formats:  (123)456-7890,  1234567890  or  123-456-
7890";
    result = false;
  }
```

Regex is a complicated subject that is out of the scope of this book. We can use a regular expression in JavaScript calling the match() function on a string value. However, note that the use of email validation with regular expression will certainly result in dropping some perfectly valid emails, so you'd better not use validation at all and rely on sending confirmation emails instead.

We get a reference to the two check box elements on the page through getElementByName(), as in the radio box case. We only have to check the first one:

```
if(checks[0].checked === false){
  acceptError.innerHTML = "You should agree to the terms";
  result = false;
}
```

Finally, we check whether the user has entered a preferred password, as well as whether the two passwords match:

```
if(password.value.length < 8){
  passwordError.innerHTML = "Password should contain at least 8 characters";
  result = false;
}
if(confirm.value !== password.value){
  confirmError.innerHTML = "Password and Confirm Password do not match";
  result = false;
}
```

You can find this project in GitHub:

https://github.com/htset/vanilla_javascript_projects/tree/main/form

11. Appointments list

In this project, we will create a web app that will store our appointments. For simplicity, each appointment will have a fixed duration of 1 hour each.

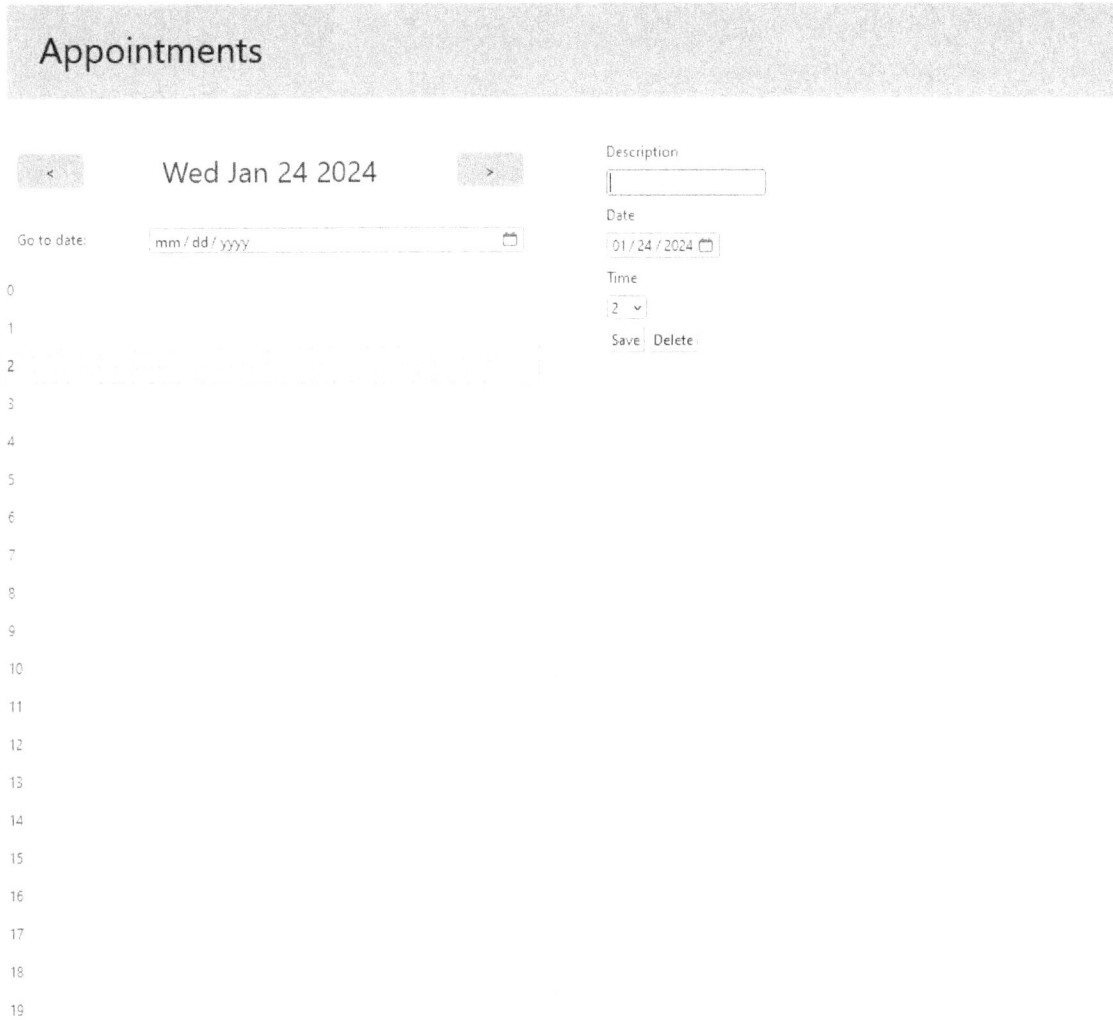

Concepts covered

- DOM manipulation
- Date handling
- Maps

Proposed Solution

Let's start with the *index.html* file:

```
<!DOCTYPE html>
<html lang="en">
```

```html
<head>
  <link
href="https://cdn.jsdelivr.net/npm/bootstrap@5.2.3/dist/css/bootstrap.min.css"
  rel="stylesheet"
  integrity="sha384-rbsA2VBKQhggwzxH7pPCaAqO46MgnOM80zW1RWuH61DGLwZJEdK2Kadq2F9CUG65"
  crossorigin="anonymous">
</head>

<body>
  <div class="container">
    <header id="main-header" class="bg-info text-black p-4 m-4">
      <div class="container">
        <h1 id="header-title">Appointments</h1>
      </div>
    </header>

    <div class="row">
      <div class="col-lg-6">
        <div class="card card-body">
          <div class="row border border-black p-3">
            <div class="col-2">
              <button class="btn btn-info w-100" id="previousDate">&lt;</button>
            </div>
            <div class="col-8">
              <h2 class="text-center" id="displayedDate"></h2>
            </div>
            <div class="col-2">
              <button class="btn btn-info w-100" id="nextDate">&gt;</button>
            </div>
          </div>
          <div class="row border border-black p-3">
            <div class="col-3">
              Go to date:
            </div>
            <div class="col-9">
              <input class="w-100" type="date" id="gotoDate" />
            </div>
          </div>

          <div class="row">
            <ul id="appointments" class="list-group">

            </ul>
          </div>
        </div>
      </div>

      <div class="col-lg-6" id="appointmentForm">
        <div class="card card-body">
          <div class="row m-1">
            <div class="col-md-4">
              <label for="apmnt_desc">Description</label>
            </div>
          </div>
```

```html
          <div class="row m-1">
            <div class="col-md-4">
              <input type="text" id="appointmentDesc" />
            </div>
          </div>
          <div class="row m-1">
            <div class="col-md-4">
              <label for="appointmentDate">Date</label>
            </div>
          </div>
          <div class="row m-1">
            <div class="col-md-4">
              <input type="date" id="appointmentDate" />
            </div>
          </div>
          <div class="row m-1">
            <div class="col-md-4">
              <label for="appointmentTime">Time</label>
            </div>
          </div>
          <div class="row m-1">
            <div class="col-md-4">
              <select id="appointmentTime"></select>
            </div>
          </div>
          <div class="row m-1">
            <div class="col-md-4">
              <button id="save">Save</button>
              <button id="delete">Delete</button>
            </div>
          </div>
        </div>
      </div>
    </div>
  </div>
  <script
  src="https://cdn.jsdelivr.net/npm/bootstrap@5.2.3/dist/js/bootstrap.bundle.min.js"
  integrity="sha384-kenU1KFdBIe4zVF0s0G1M5b4hcpxyD9F7jL+jjXkk+Q2h455rYXK/7HAuoJl+0I4"
  crossorigin="anonymous"></script>
  <script src="script.js" type="text/javascript"></script>
</body>

</html>
```

Listing 11-1: index.html

We divide the main panel of the app into two equal-sized columns, with the use of
Bootstrap:

```html
<div class="row">
  <div class="col-lg-6">
    ...
  </div>
  <div class="col-lg-6">
```

```
    ...
  </div>
</div>
```

On the left part, we have the currently selected date, broken down into hour slots. The hour slots are dynamically created as list items (<li>) using JavaScript, as we will se later on. We also have buttons to move to the next or the previous date, as well as a date picker to move to any other date.

On the right part, we will display the appointment details. There are two cases here that happen when we click on an hour slot:

- If the slot already contains an appointment, then the appointment details are loaded on the right panel. We can update the appointment details (e.g. change the date and time, or the appointment text) and press on the save button to update the appointment.
- If the slot is empty, then we can enter a new appointment by filling in the details on the right panel.

All this is performed using JavaScript; let's see the full code, before breaking it down to explain:

```javascript
const displayedDateEl = document.getElementById("displayedDate");
const previousDateEl = document.getElementById("previousDate");
const nextDateEl = document.getElementById("nextDate");
const gotoDateEl = document.getElementById("gotoDate");
const appointmentForm = document.getElementById("appointmentForm");
const appointmentsListEl = document.getElementById("appointments");
const appointmentDescEl = document.getElementById("appointmentDesc");
const appointmentDateEl = document.getElementById("appointmentDate");
const appointmentTimeEl = document.getElementById("appointmentTime");
const saveEl = document.getElementById("save");
const deleteEl = document.getElementById("delete");

//create initial appointment list
const createAppointmentList = function () {
  for (let i = 0; i < 24; i++) {
    //create <li> element
    const item = document.createElement("li");
    const textnode = document.createTextNode(i);
    item.appendChild(textnode);
    item.setAttribute("class", "list-group-item");
    item.setAttribute("id", "hour_" + i);
    item.addEventListener("click", handleClickOnHour);
    appointmentsListEl.appendChild(item);

    //create <option> for hours <select> element
    const option = document.createElement("option");
    const textnode_option = document.createTextNode(i);
    option.setAttribute("value", i);
```

```javascript
      option.appendChild(textnode_option);
      appointmentTimeEl.append(option);
   }
}

//clear appointments from list
const clearAppointmentsList = function () {
  for (let i = 0; i < 24; i++) {
    document.getElementById("hour_" + i).innerHTML = i;
    document.getElementById("hour_" + i).classList.remove("active");
  }
}

//update appointments list
const updateUI = function () {
  displayedDateEl.innerHTML = displayedDate.toDateString();

  clearAppointmentsList();

  //get appointments for displayed date
  let appointmentsInDay = appointments.get(displayedDate.toDateString());
  if (appointmentsInDay !== undefined) {
    appointmentsInDay.forEach((value, key) => {
      if (value !== undefined) {
        document.getElementById("hour_" + key).innerHTML = key + "   " + value;
        document.getElementById("hour_" + key).classList.add("active");
      }
    });
  }
}

//called when user clicks on an hour
const handleClickOnHour = function (event) {
  //remove highlight from previously selected hour
  document.getElementById("hour_" + selectedTime)
      .classList.remove("list-group-item-dark");
  selectedTime = event.target.id.substring(5, event.target.id.length);

  appointmentForm.style.visibility = "visible";

  //get appointment description from Map and display it in text box
  let tmp = appointments.get(displayedDate.toDateString());
  if (tmp !== undefined) {
    if (tmp[selectedTime] !== undefined) {
      appointmentDescEl.value = tmp[selectedTime];
      selectedDesc = tmp[selectedTime];
    }
    else {
      appointmentDescEl.value = "";
    }
  }
  else {
    appointmentDescEl.value = "";
  }
```

```javascript
    //update appointment date and time controls
    appointmentDateEl.value = getDateOnlyString(displayedDate);
    appointmentTimeEl.value = selectedTime;

    //add highlight to newly selected hour
    document.getElementById("hour_" + selectedTime)
      .classList.add("list-group-item-dark");

    appointmentDescEl.focus();
}

//update appointment when user presses save
const updateAppointment = function (appDesc, appDate, appTime) {
  if (appointments.get(appDate.toDateString()) === undefined) {
    //if there is no entry in the map for this date
    // ->we save the appointment
    appointments.set(appDate.toDateString(), new Array());
    appointments.get(appDate.toDateString())[appTime] = appDesc;
  }
  else {
    //if there is an entry in the map for this date
    // ->first check if the time is empty
    if (appointments.get(appDate.toDateString())[appTime] === undefined) {
      appointments.get(appDate.toDateString())[appTime] = appDesc;
    }
    else {
      //check if it is the same entry
      if (areDatesEqual(selectedDate, appDate)
        && selectedTime == appTime) {
        //just update description without asking user
        appointments.get(appDate.toDateString())[appTime] = appDesc;
      }
      else {
        //ask user to overwrite existing entry
        let ret = confirm("Destination date and time not empty. Overwrite?");
        if (ret) {
          //insert entry to new location
          appointments.get(appDate.toDateString())[appTime] = appDesc;
        }
        else
          return;
      }
    }
  }

  if (!areDatesEqual(selectedDate, appDate) || selectedTime != appTime) {
    //remove entry from previous location
    appointments.get(selectedDate.toDateString())[selectedTime]
      = undefined;
  }

  //if we moved the appointment to another date -> go to this date
  if (!areDatesEqual(selectedDate, appDate)) {
```

```javascript
      displayedDateTime = appDate;
      displayedDate = appDate;
      updateUI();
    }

    //remove highlight from previously selected hour
    document.getElementById("hour_" + selectedTime)
      .classList.remove("list-group-item-dark");
    selectedDate = appDate;
    selectedTime = appTime;
    //add highlight to newly selected hour
    document.getElementById("hour_" + selectedTime)
        .classList.add("list-group-item-dark");
}

//move to next date
nextDateEl.addEventListener("click", () => {
  displayedDateTime.setDate(displayedDateTime.getDate() + 1);
  displayedDate = getDateOnly(displayedDateTime);
  appointmentForm.style.visibility = "hidden";
  updateUI();
});

//move to previous date
previousDateEl.addEventListener("click", () => {
  displayedDateTime.setDate(displayedDateTime.getDate() - 1);
  displayedDate = getDateOnly(displayedDateTime);
  appointmentForm.style.visibility = "hidden";
  updateUI();
});

//select new date
gotoDateEl.addEventListener("change", () => {
  displayedDateTime = new Date(gotoDateEl.value);
  displayedDate = getDateOnly(displayedDateTime);
  appointmentForm.style.visibility = "hidden";
  updateUI();
});

//save/update appointment
saveEl.addEventListener("click", () => {
  const descr = appointmentDescEl.value;
  const dateTime = new Date(appointmentDateEl.value);
  const date = getDateOnly(dateTime);
  const time = appointmentTimeEl.value;
  updateAppointment(descr, date, time);
  updateUI();
});

//delete appointment
deleteEl.addEventListener("click", () => {
  const dateTime = new Date(appointmentDateEl.value);
  const date = getDateOnly(dateTime);
  const time = parseInt(appointmentTimeEl.value);
```

```javascript
    if (appointments.get(date.toDateString()) !== undefined) {
      appointments.get(date.toDateString())[time] = undefined;
    }

    updateUI();
    appointmentDescEl.value = "";
});

//helper function for date comparison
const areDatesEqual = function (date1, date2) {
  if (date1.getFullYear() == date2.getFullYear()
     && date1.getMonth() == date2.getMonth()
     && date1.getDate() == date2.getDate())
    return true;
  else
    return false;
}

const getDateOnlyString = function (date) {
  return date.getFullYear()
     + "-" + ("0" + (date.getMonth() + 1)).slice(-2)
     + "-" + ("0" + date.getDate()).slice(-2);
}

const getDateOnly = function (date) {
  return new Date(date.getFullYear()
     + "-" + ("0" + (date.getMonth() + 1)).slice(-2)
     + "-" + ("0" + date.getDate()).slice(-2));
}


//startup
let selectedDesc, selectedDate, selectedTime;
//appointments are stored in a map structure
let appointments = new Map();

let displayedDateTime = new Date();
let displayedDate = getDateOnly(displayedDateTime);
displayedDateEl.innerHTML = displayedDate.toDateString();


createAppointmentList();
appointmentForm.style.visibility = "hidden";

selectedDate = displayedDate;
selectedTime = 8;
```

Listing 11-2: script.js

First of all, we should note that the appointments will be stored in a Map structure. Each Map entry will be an array of strings, that will contain the text description of the appointments for a single day. For the map keys we will use the string representation of the specific date, using the toDateString() function of the Date object.

At the top of the JavaScript code, we get a reference to all the important elements of the DOM. Then, we define the `createAppointmentList()` function, which creates the unordered list that stores the appointments:

```
//create initial appointment list
const createAppointmentList = function () {
  for (let i = 0; i < 24; i++) {
    //create <li> element
    const item = document.createElement("li");
    const textnode = document.createTextNode(i);
    item.appendChild(textnode);
    item.setAttribute("class", "list-group-item");
    item.setAttribute("id", "hour_" + i);
    item.addEventListener("click", handleClickOnHour);
    appointmentsListEl.appendChild(item);

    //create <option> for hours <select> element
    const option = document.createElement("option");
    const textnode_option = document.createTextNode(i);
    option.setAttribute("value", i);
    option.appendChild(textnode_option);
    appointmentTimeEl.append(option);
  }
}
```

We see that, we create 24 `<li>` elements and their corresponding text nodes. After we apply a *class*, an *ID*, and a *listener* for the click event, we append each `<li>` element into the unordered list. Note that we apply the `list-group-item` class from Bootstrap, so the list will look like a table and not like a usual list with bullets.

Furthermore, we create the `<select>` element for the hours drop-down list of the right panel.

The function `clearAppointmentsList()` clears all entries from the list:

```
//clear appointments from list
const clearAppointmentsList = function () {
  for (let i = 0; i < 24; i++) {
    document.getElementById("hour_" + i).innerHTML = i;
    document.getElementById("hour_" + i).classList.remove("active");
  }
}
```

It also removes the `active` class from all line items. This class is used to highlight (with a blue color) the entries that contain an appointment.

Then we create the `updateUI()` function that will update the page, everytime a change has occurred:

```
//update appointments list
```

```
const updateUI = function () {
  displayedDateEl.innerHTML = displayedDate.toDateString();

  clearAppointmentsList();

  //get appointments for displayed date
  let appointmentsInDay = appointments.get(displayedDate.toDateString());
  if (appointmentsInDay !== undefined) {
    appointmentsInDay.forEach((value, key) => {
      if (value !== undefined) {
        document.getElementById("hour_" + key).innerHTML = key + "   " + value;
        document.getElementById("hour_" + key).classList.add("active");
      }
    });
  }
}
```

In updateUI(), we clear the appointment list and then we insert the appointments of the selected date in their respective slot. In order to achieve this, we first get the string array of the appointments for the selected date from the appointments Map:

```
let appointmentsInDay = appointments.get(displayedDate.toDateString());
```

Then, we perform a loop over this array, and we insert each appointment in the respective slot:

```
document.getElementById("hour_" + key).innerHTML = key + "   " + value;
document.getElementById("hour_" + key).classList.add("active");
```

The handleClickOnHour() function is called when the user clicks on an hour slot on the left panel. It first removes the grey highlight from the previously selected slot. Then, it gets the newly selected time from the clicked item's ID:

```
selectedTime = event.target.id.substring(5, event.target.id.length);
```

Note that each <li> element has an ID of the type *hour_X*, where X is the specific time.

Next, we display the right panel; this panel is by default hidden and it will appear when the user clicks on a time slot. When the user changes the selected date, the right panel will be hidden again.

Afterwards, we get the appointment of the selected date and time (if any), and we update the controls of the right panel accordingly.

Finally, we highlight the newly selected hour with a grey color, and we give the focus to the description text box.

When the user presses the Save button, the `updateAppoinment()` function is called:

```
//update appointment when user presses save
const updateAppointment = function (appDesc, appDate, appTime) {
  if (appointments.get(appDate.toDateString()) === undefined) {
    //if there is no entry in the map for this date
    // ->we save the appointment
    appointments.set(appDate.toDateString(), new Array());
    appointments.get(appDate.toDateString())[appTime] = appDesc;
  }
  else {
    //if there is an entry in the map for this date
    // ->first check if the time is empty
    if (appointments.get(appDate.toDateString())[appTime] === undefined) {
      appointments.get(appDate.toDateString())[appTime] = appDesc;
    }
    else {
      //check if it is the same entry
      if (areDatesEqual(selectedDate, appDate)
        && selectedTime == appTime) {
        //just update description without asking user
        appointments.get(appDate.toDateString())[appTime] = appDesc;
      }
      else {
        //ask user to overwrite existing entry
        let ret = confirm("Destination date and time not empty. Overwrite?");
        if (ret) {
          //insert entry to new location
          appointments.get(appDate.toDateString())[appTime] = appDesc;
        }
        else
          return;
      }
    }
  }

  if (!areDatesEqual(selectedDate, appDate) || selectedTime != appTime) {
    //remove entry from previous location
    appointments.get(selectedDate.toDateString())[selectedTime]
      = undefined;
  }

  //if we moved the appointment to another date -> go to this date
  if (!areDatesEqual(selectedDate, appDate)) {
    displayedDateTime = appDate;
    displayedDate = appDate;
    updateUI();
  }

  //remove highlight from previously selected hour
  document.getElementById("hour_" + selectedTime)
    .classList.remove("list-group-item-dark");
  selectedDate = appDate;
  selectedTime = appTime;
```

```
//add highlight to newly selected hour
  document.getElementById("hour_"   +   selectedTime).classList.add("list-group-item-
dark");
}
```

This function handles a combination of cases:

- A new appointment is entered, or an existing one is updated. In the latter case, we will have to remove the previous entry from the list.
- The appointment is entered in an empty slot, or there is already an existing entry there. In the latter case, we will have to confirm with the user that the existing entry should be overwritten.

Finally, if the entry was created on another date, then we should move to this date. This means that the currently displayed date will change, and that the UI should be updated accordingly.

Next, we define a series of event listeners. The first 3 listeners handle a change in the selected date, while the latter 2 listeners handle the insertion/update and delete actions of the user.

The last 3 functions are helper functions: function areDatesEqual() checks for date equality. We have to make such a function ourselves, as there is no such functionality available for the Date object.

The getDateOnlyString() function gives us a string representation of the date only (without time). We take special care for the preceeding zeros in the days and months values that are below 10. The getDateOnly() function gives us a Date object where the time portion is 00:00:00. This is helpful because when we get the current Date with:

```
let d = new Date();
```

we also get the current time.

Finally, at the end of the script file, we initialize the Map structure and the appointment list.

You can find this project in GitHub:

https://github.com/htset/vanilla_javascript_projects/tree/main/appointments1

12. Appointments list (version 2)

Continuing with the appointment list project, we will refactor the web app by separating the UI-specific code and the business logic. We will also employ centralized state management functionality, using functional programming concepts. In this way, we aim to make the web app easier to test.

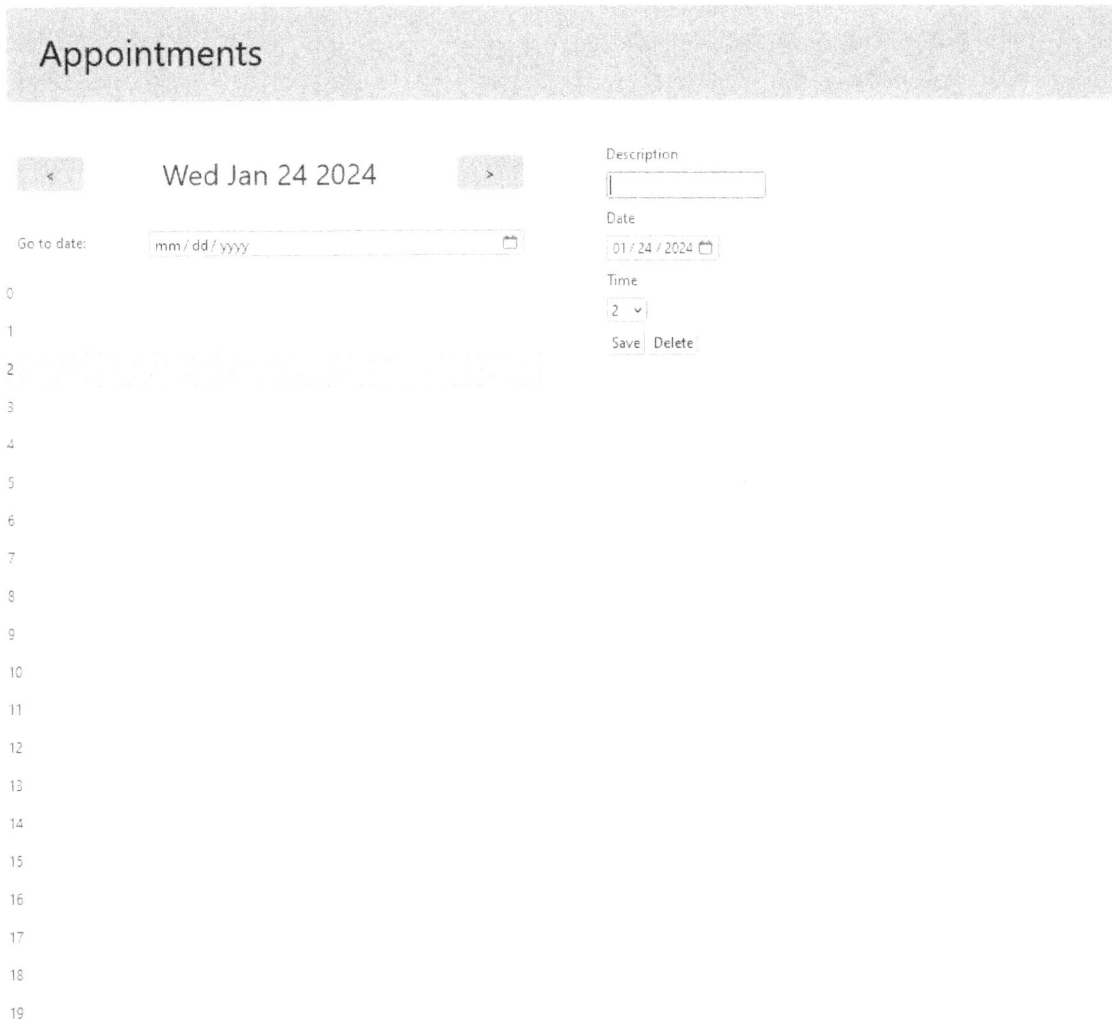

Concepts covered

- Functional programming
- State management

Proposed Solution

In the first version of the appointments list web app, we were mixing *UI functionality* and *business logic* at many places in our code. With the term *UI functionality* we refer to code that handles interaction with the user (event handlers) and updates the user interface (such as the `updateUI()` function). Conversely, wih the term *business logic*, we refer to the code that mainly performs calculations, as in our case is the insertion or the deletion of an appointment in the appointments list.

The mixing of those two types of functionalities means that our code cannot be easily tested. We need to separate the UI and the business logic into distinct functions so that we can perform the testing of our business logic.

In version 1, we defined some variables (e.g. `displayedDate`, `selectedDesc`, etc.) that contained the application state. However, this state was being *mutated*, i.e. we changed their value directly. In this version, we will employ state management techniques: we will gather all state variables in one big state object, and we will create business logic functions that do not mutate the state, but instead return a new state object every time.

The application state is created at the bottom of the JavaScript file as follows:

```
let state = {
  appointments: new Map(),
  displayedDate: getDateOnly(d),
  selectedDesc: "",
  selectedDate: getDateOnly(d),
  selectedTime: 8,
  selectedVisible: false
};
```

Listing 12-1: script.js

We see that the state contains the `appointments` list and the currently `displayedDate`. It also contains the variables that control the elements of the right panel (`selectedDesc`, `selectedDate`, `selectedTime`). Finally, boolean variable `selectedVisible` controls whether the right panel wil be visible or not.

Let's start with our *index.html* file. It will not be changed and is presented here for completeness:

```
<!DOCTYPE html>
<html lang="en">

<head>
  <link
href="https://cdn.jsdelivr.net/npm/bootstrap@5.2.3/dist/css/bootstrap.min.css"
  rel="stylesheet"
  integrity="sha384-rbsA2VBKQhggwzxH7pPCaAqO46MgnOM80zW1RWuH61DGLwZJEdK2Kadq2F9CUG65"
  crossorigin="anonymous">
</head>

<body>
  <div class="container">
    <header id="main-header" class="bg-info text-black p-4 m-4">
      <div class="container">
        <h1 id="header-title">Appointments</h1>
```

```
      </div>
  </header>

<div class="row">
   <div class="col-lg-6">
      <div class="card card-body">
         <div class="row border border-black p-3">
            <div class="col-2">
               <button class="btn btn-info w-100" id="previousDate">&lt;</button>
            </div>
            <div class="col-8">
               <h2 class="text-center" id="displayedDate"></h2>
            </div>
            <div class="col-2">
               <button class="btn btn-info w-100" id="nextDate">&gt;</button>
            </div>
         </div>
         <div class="row border border-black p-3">
            <div class="col-3">
               Go to date:
            </div>
            <div class="col-9">
               <input class="w-100" type="date" id="gotoDate" />
            </div>
         </div>

         <div class="row">
            <ul id="appointments" class="list-group">

            </ul>
         </div>
      </div>
   </div>

   <div class="col-lg-6" id="appointmentForm">
      <div class="card card-body">
         <div class="row m-1">
            <div class="col-md-4">
               <label for="apmnt_desc">Description</label>
            </div>
         </div>
         <div class="row m-1">
            <div class="col-md-4">
               <input type="text" id="appointmentDesc" />
            </div>
         </div>
         <div class="row m-1">
            <div class="col-md-4">
               <label for="appointmentDate">Date</label>
            </div>
         </div>
         <div class="row m-1">
            <div class="col-md-4">
               <input type="date" id="appointmentDate" />
```

```html
          </div>
        </div>
        <div class="row m-1">
          <div class="col-md-4">
            <label for="appointmentTime">Time</label>
          </div>
        </div>
        <div class="row m-1">
          <div class="col-md-4">
            <select id="appointmentTime"></select>
          </div>
        </div>
        <div class="row m-1">
          <div class="col-md-4">
            <button id="save">Save</button>
            <button id="delete">Delete</button>
          </div>
        </div>
      </div>
    </div>
  </div>
</div>
<script
src="https://cdn.jsdelivr.net/npm/bootstrap@5.2.3/dist/js/bootstrap.bundle.min.js"
integrity="sha384-kenU1KFdBIe4zVF0s0G1M5b4hcpxyD9F7jL+jjXkk+Q2h455rYXK/7HAuoJl+0I4"
crossorigin="anonymous"></script>
<script src="script.js" type="text/javascript"></script>
</body>

</html>
```

Listing 12-2: index.html

The JavaScript file is becoming quite long, so we will examine it block by block. First the elements declaration:

```javascript
const displayedDateEl = document.getElementById("displayedDate");
const previousDateEl = document.getElementById("previousDate");
const nextDateEl = document.getElementById("nextDate");
const gotoDateEl = document.getElementById("gotoDate");
const appointmentForm = document.getElementById("appointmentForm");
const appointmentsListEl = document.getElementById("appointments");
const appointmentDescEl = document.getElementById("appointmentDesc");
const appointmentDateEl = document.getElementById("appointmentDate");
const appointmentTimeEl = document.getElementById("appointmentTime");
const saveEl = document.getElementById("save");
const deleteEl = document.getElementById("delete");
```

Listing 12-3: script.js

Then, we define the UI-specific functions:

```javascript
//create initial appointment list
const createAppointmentList = function () {
```

```javascript
  for (let i = 0; i < 24; i++) {
    //create <li> element
    const item = document.createElement("li");
    const textnode = document.createTextNode(i);
    item.appendChild(textnode);
    item.setAttribute("class", "list-group-item");
    item.setAttribute("id", "hour_" + i);
    item.addEventListener("click", handleClickOnHour);
    appointmentsListEl.appendChild(item);

    //create <option> for hours <select> element
    const option = document.createElement("option");
    const textnode_option = document.createTextNode(i);
    option.setAttribute("value", i);
    option.appendChild(textnode_option);
    appointmentTimeEl.append(option);
  }
}

//clear appointments from list
const clearAppointmentsList = function () {
  for (let i = 0; i < 24; i++) {
    document.getElementById("hour_" + i).innerHTML = i;
    document.getElementById("hour_" + i).classList.remove("active");
  }
}

//update appointments list
const updateUI = function (state) {
  displayedDateEl.innerHTML = state.displayedDate.toDateString();
  appointmentDescEl.value = state.selectedDesc;
  appointmentDateEl.value = getDateOnlyString(state.selectedDate);
  appointmentTimeEl.value = state.selectedTime;
  appointmentFormEl.style.visibility   =   (state.selectedVisible)   ?   "visible"   :
"hidden";

  clearAppointmentsList();

  //get appointments for displayed date
  let appointmentsInDay = state.appointments.get(state.displayedDate.toDateString());
  if (appointmentsInDay !== undefined) {
    appointmentsInDay.forEach((value, key) => {
      if (value !== undefined) {
        document.getElementById("hour_" + key).innerHTML = key + "   " + value;
        document.getElementById("hour_" + key).classList.add("active");
      }
    });
  }
  for (let i = 0; i < 24; i++) {
    document.getElementById("hour_" + i)
      .classList.remove("list-group-item-dark");
  }
  document.getElementById("hour_" + state.selectedTime)
    .classList.add("list-group-item-dark");
```

```
}
```
Listing 12-4: script.js

The createAppointmentList() and clearAppointmentList() functions are unchanged. The updateUI() function is modified to use the state object in order to update the various elements of the user interface (including the appointments list).

Next, we proceed with the event handlers:

```
//called when user clicks on an hour
const handleClickOnHour = function (event) {
  state = selectSlot(state, event.target.id.substring(5, event.target.id.length));
  updateUI(state);
  appointmentDescEl.focus();
}

//move to next date
const handleNext = function() {
  state = addDaysToDate(state, 1);
  updateUI(state);
}

//move to previous date
const handlePrevious = function() {
  state = addDaysToDate(state, -1);
  updateUI(state);
}

//select new date
const handleGoto = function() {
  let newDateTime = new Date(gotoDateEl.value);
  state = updateDisplayedDate(state, newDateTime);
  updateUI(state);
}

//save/update appointment
const handleSave = function() {
  const newDescr = appointmentDescEl.value;
  const dateTime = new Date(appointmentDateEl.value);
  const newDate = getDateOnly(dateTime);
  const newTime = appointmentTimeEl.value;

  if (slotAlreadyTaken(state, newDate, newTime)
    && !(areDatesEqual(state.selectedDate, newDate)
          && state.selectedTime == newTime)) {
    //ask user to overwrite existing entry
    let ret = confirm("Destination date and time not empty. Overwrite?");
    if (ret) {
      //insert entry to new location
      state = updateAppointment(state, newDescr, newDate, newTime);
      updateUI(state);
    }
  }
  else {
```

```
    //insert entry to new location
    state = updateAppointment(state, newDescr, newDate, newTime);
    updateUI(state);
  }
}

//delete appointment
const handleDelete = function() {
  const dateTime = new Date(appointmentDateEl.value);
  const date = getDateOnly(dateTime);
  const time = parseInt(appointmentTimeEl.value);
  state = deleteAppointment(state, date, time);
  updateUI(state);
}
```

Listing 12-5: script.js

The event handler functions are called to handle user-generated events, such as moving to the next date, or pressing the save button. In essence, those functions retrieve the values of the elements (such as the appointment description, or the number of the clicked time slot) and pass them to the business logic functions. Then, they get the updated application state and they use it to update UI, by calling the updateUI() function.

The business logic functions are next:

```
//checks whether a time slot is already occupied
const slotAlreadyTaken = function (state, date, time) {
  if (state.appointments.get(date.toDateString()) !== undefined
      && state.appointments.get(date.toDateString()).get(time) !== undefined)
    return true;
  else
    return false;
}

//update appointment when user presses save
const updateAppointment = function (state, newDesc, newDate, newTime) {
  let newAppointments = new Map();
  state.appointments.forEach((value, key) => {
    newAppointments.set(key, new Map());
    state.appointments.get(key).forEach((v, k) => {
      if (!(state.selectedDate.toDateString() == key && state.selectedTime == k)) {
        newAppointments.get(key).set(k, state.appointments.get(key).get(k));
      }
    });
  });

  if (!newAppointments.has(newDate.toDateString())) {
    newAppointments.set(newDate.toDateString(), new Map());
  }
  newAppointments.get(newDate.toDateString()).set(newTime, newDesc);

  let newState = {
    appointments: newAppointments,
```

```
      displayedDate: newDate,
      selectedDesc: newDesc,
      selectedDate: newDate,
      selectedTime: newTime,
      selectedVisible: state.selectedVisible
  }

  return newState;
}

const deleteAppointment = function (state, date, time) {
  let newAppointments = new Map();
  state.appointments.forEach((value, key) => {
    newAppointments.set(key, new Map());
    state.appointments.get(key).forEach((v, k) => {
      if (!(date.toDateString() == key && time == k)) {
        newAppointments.get(key).set(k, state.appointments.get(key).get(k));
      }
    });
  });

  let newState = {
    appointments: newAppointments,
    displayedDate: state.displayedDate,
    selectedDesc: "",
    selectedDate: state.selectedDate,
    selectedTime: state.selectedTime,
    selectedVisible: state.selectedVisible
  }

  return newState;
}

//called when the user clicks on a time slot
const selectSlot = function (state, newTime) {
  let newDesc;

  //get appmt description from Map and display it in text box
  let tmp = state.appointments.get(state.displayedDate.toDateString());
  if (tmp !== undefined) {
    if (tmp.get(newTime) !== undefined) {
      newDesc = tmp.get(newTime);
    }
    else {
      newDesc = "";
    }
  }
  else {
    newDesc = "";
  }

  let newState = {
    appointments: state.appointments,
    displayedDate: state.displayedDate,
```

```
      selectedDesc: newDesc,
      selectedDate: state.displayedDate,
      selectedTime: newTime,
      selectedVisible: true
   }

   return newState;
}

//update the displayedDate variable
const updateDisplayedDate = function(state, newDate){
   let newDisplayedDate = getDateOnly(newDate);

   let newState = {
      appointments: state.appointments,
      displayedDate: newDisplayedDate,
      selectedDesc: state.selectedDesc,
      selectedDate: newDisplayedDate,
      selectedTime: state.selectedTime,
      selectedVisible: false
   }
   return newState;
}

//increase/descrease displayedDate
const addDaysToDate = function(state, days){
   let newDisplayedDate = state.displayedDate;
   newDisplayedDate.setDate(state.displayedDate.getDate() + days);

   let newState = {
      appointments: state.appointments,
      displayedDate: newDisplayedDate,
      selectedDesc: state.selectedDesc,
      selectedDate: state.selectedDate,
      selectedTime: state.selectedTime,
      selectedVisible: false
   }
   return newState;
}
```
Listing 12-6: script.js

First of all, note that we changed the internal workings of the appointments Map: now we have another Map object instead of an array, to represent the hours within a specific date. So now, the appointments Map contains Map objects instead of arrays.

As already mentioned, the main responsibility of those functions is to update the application state by applying the business logic rules. Following the *Functional Programming* tenets, we do not mutate the application state, but we create a new state object.

For instance, in the updateAppointment() function, we create a new Map, by copying the appointments from the existing Map. In the case of appointment update, we make sure we add the appointment under a new key in the Map, and that we do not copy the old entry into the new Map.

All business logic functions return the newly created application state object. This object is used by the UI to update the elements in the DOM.

Next, we have the helper functions, unchanged from version 1:

```
//helper function for date comparison
const areDatesEqual = function (date1, date2) {
  if (date1.getFullYear() == date2.getFullYear()
    && date1.getMonth() == date2.getMonth()
    && date1.getDate() == date2.getDate())
    return true;
  else
    return false;
}

const getDateOnlyString = function (date) {
  return date.getFullYear()
    + "-" + ("0" + (date.getMonth() + 1)).slice(-2)
    + "-" + ("0" + date.getDate()).slice(-2);
}

const getDateOnly = function (date) {
  return new Date(date.getFullYear()
    + "-" + ("0" + (date.getMonth() + 1)).slice(-2)
    + "-" + ("0" + date.getDate()).slice(-2));
}
```

Listing 12-7: script.js

The event listeners are presented next:

```
nextDateEl.addEventListener("click", handleNext);
previousDateEl.addEventListener("click", handlePrevious);
gotoDateEl.addEventListener("change", handleGoto);
saveEl.addEventListener("click", handleSave);
deleteEl.addEventListener("click", handleDelete);
```

Listing 12-8: script.js

And finally, the code that will run on startup:

```
let d = new Date();
let state = {
  appointments: new Map(),
  displayedDate: getDateOnly(d),
  selectedDesc: "",
  selectedDate: getDateOnly(d),
  selectedTime: 8,
  selectedVisible: false
};
```

```
createAppointmentList();
updateUI(state);
```

Listing 12-9: script.js

We see that we create the application state object and that we use it to update the UI.

In the next project, we will employ *unit testing* in our application, to make sure that our business logic works as expected.

You can find this project in GitHub:

https://github.com/htset/vanilla_javascript_projects/tree/main/appointments2

13. Appointments list (version 3)

For this project, we will introduce Uniy Testing for the business logic and helper functions of our web app.

QUnit Test Suite

Hide passed tests Check for Globals No try-catch   Filter: [   ] Go   Module: [All modules ▼]

QUnit 2.20.0; Mozilla/5.0 (Windows NT 10.0; Win64; x64; rv:121.0) Gecko/20100101 Firefox/121.0

7 tests completed in 2972 milliseconds, with 0 failed, 0 skipped, and 0 todo.
10 assertions of 10 passed, 0 failed.

1. Logic testing: When user clicks on an hour slot - the right panel is updated (3) Rerun   2943 ms
2. Helpers testing: When dates are not equal - areDatesEqual() returns false (1) Rerun   2 ms
3. Helpers testing: When dates are equal - areDatesEqual() returns true (1) Rerun   3 ms
4. Logic testing: When appointment already exists at specific date and time - slotAlreadyTaken() returns true (1) Rerun   4 ms
5. Logic testing: When appointment does not exist at specific date and time - slotAlreadyTaken() returns false (1) Rerun   3 ms
6. Logic testing: When updating existing appointment to a new date - the existing one is removed (2) Rerun   2 ms
7. Logic testing: When deleting appointment - the appointment is removed (1) Rerun   1 ms

Concepts covered

- Unit testing (QUnit)
- Use of multiple JS files

Proposed Solution

We will use QUnit (https://qunitjs.com/), a very simple testing framework, that can be employed to test JavaScript code on the client-side (i.e. web browser), as well as on the server-side (i.e. Node.js). It is very easy to use QUnit; it requires minimal configuration for testing browser-based projects, as in our case.

First of all, we should note that, in order to facilitate Unit Testing, we have broken the original JavaScript file (*script.js*) into three files:

- *helpers.js* (the helper functions)
- *logic.js* (the business logic)
- *ui.js* (the UI code and the event handlers)

We have also updated the *index.html* file to load all three files:

```
<script src="helpers.js" type="text/javascript"></script>
<script src="logic.js" type="text/javascript"></script>
<script src="ui.js" type="text/javascript"></script>
```

Listing 13-1: index.html

The order that those scripts are loaded is important. First, we load the helper functions, since they are used in the other two files. Then we load the business logic, and at the end we load the UI code. If we did not load the helper functions at the start, those functions

---

81

would not be available when loading the other two scripts, as the scripts are loaded sequentially.

We will use QUnit to unit test the former two files. The UI code can be tested in Functional and End-To-End tests, where we test the web application as a whole, using testing frameworks like Selenium, Cypress or Playright.

In order to use QUnit, we have to create a new HTML file that will load the QUnit framework as well as the code to test:

```
<!DOCTYPE html>
<meta charset="utf-8">
<title>QUnit Test Suite</title>
<link rel="stylesheet" href="https://code.jquery.com/qunit/qunit-2.20.0.css">
<body>
  <div id="qunit"></div>
  <div id="qunit-fixture"></div>
  <script src="https://code.jquery.com/qunit/qunit-2.20.0.js"></script>
  <script src="helpers.js" type="text/javascript"></script>
  <script src="logic.js" type="text/javascript"></script>
  <script src="tests.js" type="text/javascript"></script>
</body>
```

Listing 13-2: test_qunit.html

We can run our tests simply by loading this page in our web browser.

We see that our HTML file loads a JavaScript and a CSS file from the JQuery web site (QUnit was actually created for JQuery testing initially). It also loads three JavaScript files:

- *helpers.js*
- *logic.js*
- *tests.js* (the unit tests)

The unit tests file consists of two QUnit modules, one for each file under test. The first module contains the tests for the helper functions:

```
QUnit.module('Helpers testing', function() {
  QUnit.test('When dates are not equal - areDatesEqual() returns false',
    function(assert) {
    let d1 = new Date(2023, 12, 31);
    let d2 = new Date(2023, 12, 30);

    assert.equal(areDatesEqual(d1, d2), false);
  });

  QUnit.test('When dates are equal - areDatesEqual() returns true',
    function(assert){
    let d1 = new Date(2023, 12, 31);
    let d2 = new Date(2023, 12, 31);

    assert.equal(areDatesEqual(d1, d2), true);
```

```
  });
});
```

Listing 13-3: tests.js

Here, we have two tests for the `areDatesEqual()` function. We create two `Date` objects and we pass them to this function. The returned boolean result of this function is compared to the expected value in the `assert.equal()` function.

If the two values do not match then the test fails, and we get red color in the testing web page (*test_qunit.html*):

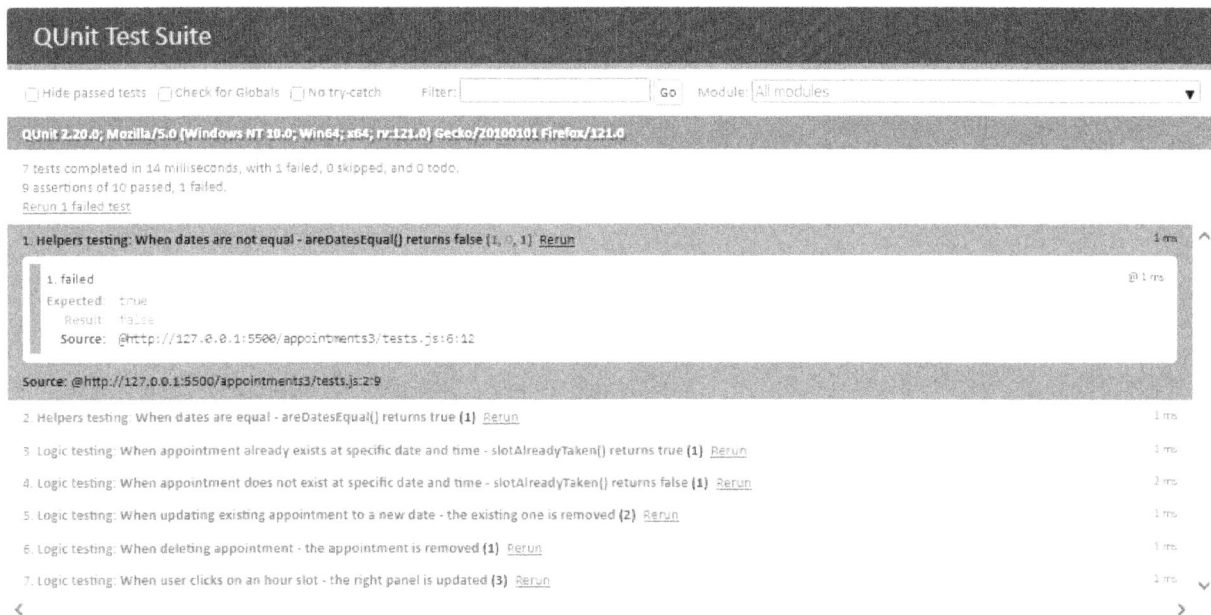

Note that we can understand which tests failed from the descriptions that we passed on the QUnit module and the specific test. For this reason, we should try to be a descriptive as possible when providing descriptions for tests, as it will make our life easier. In the above image, we can see that the failed test is the "*When dates are not equal - areDatesEqual() returns false*" in the "*Helpers testing*" unit.

Now, let's see the second QUnit module, that is used for testing business logic:

```
QUnit.module('Logic testing', function() {
  QUnit.test('When  appointment  already  exists  at  specific  date  and  time  -
slotAlreadyTaken() returns true', function(assert) {
    let d = new Date(2024, 1, 10);
    let map = new Map();
    let day = new Map();
    day.set(10, "test");
    map.set(d.toDateString(), day);
    let state = {
      appointments: map,
```

```
      displayedDate: getDateOnly(d),
      selectedDesc: "",
      selectedDate: getDateOnly(d),
      selectedTime: 8,
      selectedVisible: false
   };

   assert.equal(slotAlreadyTaken(state, d, 10), true);
 });

 QUnit.test('When appointment does not exist at specific date and time -
slotAlreadyTaken() returns false', function(assert) {
     let d = new Date(2024, 1, 10);
     let map = new Map();
     let day = new Map();
     day.set(10, "test");
     map.set(d.toDateString(), day);
     let state = {
       appointments: map,
       displayedDate: getDateOnly(d),
       selectedDesc: "",
       selectedDate: getDateOnly(d),
       selectedTime: 8,
       selectedVisible: false
   };

   assert.equal(slotAlreadyTaken(state, d, 9), false);
 });

...
```

Listing 13-4: tests.js

First we test the slotAlreadyTaken() function. We set the application state that is active at the start of the test. More specifically, we add an appointment on February 10, 2024 at 10:00. Then we call the slotAlreadyTaken() function to test whether this date and time is already occupied. The function should return true, and the test should pass.

On the second test, we aim to verify that this function would return false, for a time slot that is not currently occupied.

Next, we test the updateAppointment() function:

```
QUnit.test('When updating existing appointment to a new date - the existing one is
removed', function(assert) {
    let d = new Date(2024, 1, 10);
    let d2 = new Date(2024, 1, 11);
    let map = new Map();
    let day = new Map();
    day.set(10, "test");
    map.set(d.toDateString(), day);
    let state = {
      appointments: map,
      displayedDate: getDateOnly(d),
      selectedDesc: "",
      selectedDate: getDateOnly(d),
      selectedTime: 10,
      selectedVisible: false
    };

    let newState = updateAppointment(state, "test", d2, 7);
    assert.equal(newState.appointments.get(d2.toDateString()).get(7), "test");
    assert.equal(newState.appointments.get(d.toDateString()).has(10), false);
  });
```

Here we make two asserts, one to test whether the new value has been inserted into the
appointments list, and one to verify that the old entry was indeed removed from the
application state.

Afterwards, we test the deleteAppointment() function.

```
  QUnit.test('When      deleting    appointment     -    the    appointment    is    removed',
function(assert) {
    let d = new Date(2024, 1, 10);
    let map = new Map();
    let day = new Map();
    day.set(10, "test");
    map.set(d.toDateString(), day);
    let state = {
      appointments: map,
      displayedDate: getDateOnly(d),
      selectedDesc: "",
      selectedDate: getDateOnly(d),
      selectedTime: 10,
      selectedVisible: false
    };

    let newState = deleteAppointment(state, d, 10);
    assert.equal(newState.appointments.get(d.toDateString()).has(10), false);
  });
```

Finally, we test the selectSlot() function:

```
QUnit.test('When user clicks on an hour slot - the right panel is updated',
  function(assert) {
    let d = new Date(2024, 1, 10);
    let map = new Map();
    let day = new Map();
    day.set(10, "test");
    map.set(d.toDateString(), day);
    let state = {
      appointments: map,
      displayedDate: getDateOnly(d),
      selectedDesc: "",
      selectedDate: getDateOnly(d),
      selectedTime: 8,
      selectedVisible: false
    };

    let newState = selectSlot(state, 10);
    assert.equal(newState.selectedDesc, "test");
    assert.equal(areDatesEqual(newState.selectedDate, getDateOnly(d)), true);
    assert.equal(newState.selectedTime, 10);
  });
```

Listing 13-7: tests.js

All tests follow the same pattern, *Arrange, Act and Assert (AAA)*: First we *arrange* the application state, then we *act* on it by calling the code under test and finally we *assert* over the results.

Needless to say, that the aforementioned unit tests are not adequate; we need to add more tests so that we can be certain that our application works as intended. This task is left to the reader.

In the next project, we will introduce more advanced testing capabilities using *Jest*.

You can find this project in GitHub:

https://github.com/htset/vanilla_javascript_projects/tree/main/appointments3

14. Appointments list (version 4)

We will refactor the whole web, so that it uses Webpack for bundling, Babel for ES6 support and Jest for testing.

Concepts covered

- ES6 modules
- Webpack
- Babel
- Jest

Proposed Solution

The web app that we created in the previous project is in good shape. We have separated the various functionalities into different JS files, and we have introduced testing with QUnit. However, it does not take advantage of the modern technologies that have been introduced in the JavaScript world.

More specifically, the way the JS code is loaded results in creating global objects that pollute the application namespace. This may result in conflicts between objects when multiple libraries are used. We can solve this issue by creating ES6 modules that will contain our code without creating global objects.

Moreover, in our current project we are not able to take advantage of the many libraries that have been developed for Node.js. The only libraries that we can use right now, are those that can be loaded by the browser through a link (like QUnit or Bootstrap). In order to use the NPM libraries, we will need to use a builder utility like Webpack or Vite.

By using Webpack, we can break our code into multiple modules, without creating global objects and without worrying about which file will load first. Furthermore, we can bundle those JS files into one big file that will be downloaded by the user's browser.

In this way, we can also use more advanced libraries for testing, such as *Jest*.

Part A – ES6 modules and Webpack

First of all, we have to install Node.js in our development machine. We can find it at: https://nodejs.org/en

We can then start with project initialization by typing in a command prompt:

```
npm init
```

This will create a new project, which is defined by a *package.json* file.

In the wizard, we provide the following answers:

- Package name: *appointments*
- Entry point: *ui.js*
- Test command: *jest*

We keep the default settings for the other parameters. The resulting *package.json* file will look like the following:

```
{
  "name": "appointments",
  "version": "1.0.0",
  "description": "",
  "main": "ui.js",
  "scripts": {
    "test": "jest"
  },
  "author": "",
  "license": "ISC"
}
```

Listing 14-1: package.json

Next, we install the required dependencies for webpack:

```
npm install webpack webpack-cli webpack-dev-server --save-dev
```

This command will install *webpack*, *webpack-cli* and *webpack-dev-server* as development dependencies in our project. Note the *node_modules* folder that was created; it contains all the code necessary for webpack to work.

In the resulting *package.json* file we should add two entries in the "scripts" section, one for running the development server ("start") and one to build the *bundle.js* file ("build"):

```
{
  "name": "appointments",
  "version": "1.0.0",
  "description": "",
  "main": "ui.js",
  "scripts": {
    "build": "webpack",
    "start": "webpack serve --open",
    "test": "jest"
  },
  "author": "",
  "license": "ISC",
  "devDependencies": {
    "@babel/core": "^7.23.7",
    "@babel/preset-env": "^7.23.8",
    "babel-loader": "^9.1.3",
    "webpack": "^5.89.0",
    "webpack-cli": "^5.1.4",
    "webpack-dev-server": "^4.15.1"
```

```
      }
}
```
Listing 14-2: package.json

When running the *start* option (with `npm start`) then a development server is launched and a new browser window is opened loading our *index.html* file. The *build* option (with `npm run build`), creates the production ready *bundle.js* file and stores it in the *dist* folder.

Next, we should create the Webpack configuration file named *webpack.config.js* inside the root folder with the following content:

```
const path = require('path');

module.exports = {
  "mode": "none",
  "entry": "./src/ui.js",
  "output": {
    "path": __dirname + '/dist',
    "filename": "bundle.js"
  },
  devServer: {
    static: path.join(__dirname, 'public/'),
    devMiddleware: {
      publicPath: '/dist/'
    },
    port: 3000,
    hot: "only"
  }
}
```
Listing 14-3: webpack.config.js

The configuration file says that the JavaScript entry file (the file that should run first) is *ui.js* in *src* folder. It also says that all JS files will be bundled in file *bundle.js*, created in the *dist* folder.

Now, we should go ahead and create those two folders. We will also create another folder (*public*) where our *index.html* file will reside.

```
mkdir src
mkdir dist
mkdir public
```

Now, let's move the *index.html* file into the *public* folder. We will change the `<script>` elements so that they now point to the bundled JS file that we will eventually create via webpack.

```
<!DOCTYPE html>
<html lang="en">

<head>
```

```html
    <link
href="https://cdn.jsdelivr.net/npm/bootstrap@5.2.3/dist/css/bootstrap.min.css"
  rel="stylesheet"
  integrity="sha384-rbsA2VBKQhggwzxH7pPCaAqO46MgnOM80zW1RWuH61DGLwZJEdK2Kadq2F9CUG65"
  crossorigin="anonymous">
</head>

<body>
  <div class="container">
    <header id="main-header" class="bg-info text-black p-4 m-4">
      <div class="container">
        <h1 id="header-title">Appointments</h1>
      </div>
    </header>

    <div class="row">
      <div class="col-lg-6">
        <div class="card card-body">
          <div class="row border border-black p-3">
            <div class="col-2">
              <button class="btn btn-info w-100" id="previousDate">&lt;</button>
            </div>
            <div class="col-8">
              <h2 class="text-center" id="displayedDate"></h2>
            </div>
            <div class="col-2">
              <button class="btn btn-info w-100" id="nextDate">&gt;</button>
            </div>
          </div>
          <div class="row border border-black p-3">
            <div class="col-3">
              Go to date:
            </div>
            <div class="col-9">
              <input class="w-100" type="date" id="gotoDate" />
            </div>
          </div>

          <div class="row">
            <ul id="appointments" class="list-group">

            </ul>
          </div>
        </div>
      </div>

      <div class="col-lg-6" id="appointmentForm">
        <div class="card card-body">
          <div class="row m-1">
            <div class="col-md-4">
              <label for="apmnt_desc">Description</label>
            </div>
          </div>
          <div class="row m-1">
```

```html
          <div class="col-md-4">
            <input type="text" id="appointmentDesc" />
          </div>
        </div>
        <div class="row m-1">
          <div class="col-md-4">
            <label for="appointmentDate">Date</label>
          </div>
        </div>
        <div class="row m-1">
          <div class="col-md-4">
            <input type="date" id="appointmentDate" />
          </div>
        </div>
        <div class="row m-1">
          <div class="col-md-4">
            <label for="appointmentTime">Time</label>
          </div>
        </div>
        <div class="row m-1">
          <div class="col-md-4">
            <select id="appointmentTime"></select>
          </div>
        </div>
        <div class="row m-1">
          <div class="col-md-4">
            <button id="save">Save</button>
            <button id="delete">Delete</button>
          </div>
        </div>
      </div>
    </div>
  </div>
</div>
<script
src="https://cdn.jsdelivr.net/npm/bootstrap@5.2.3/dist/js/bootstrap.bundle.min.js"
integrity="sha384-kenU1KFdBIe4zVF0s0G1M5b4hcpxyD9F7jL+jjXkk+Q2h455rYXK/7HAuoJl+0I4"
crossorigin="anonymous"></script>
<script src="../dist/bundle.js"></script>
</body>

</html>
```

Listing 14-4: tests.js

We also create the 3 JS files into the *src* folder. We will have to refactor them so that they are using ES6 modules:

```
/////////////////////////////////////////////////
///  Helper Functions
/////////////////////////////////////////////////

//helper function for date comparison
export const areDatesEqual = function (date1, date2) {
  if (date1.getFullYear() == date2.getFullYear()
    && date1.getMonth() == date2.getMonth()
    && date1.getDate() == date2.getDate())
    return true;
  else
    return false;
}

export const getDateOnlyString = function (date) {
  return date.getFullYear()
    + "-" + ("0" + (date.getMonth() + 1)).slice(-2)
    + "-" + ("0" + date.getDate()).slice(-2);
}

export const getDateOnly = function (date) {
  return new Date(date.getFullYear()
    + "-" + ("0" + (date.getMonth() + 1)).slice(-2)
    + "-" + ("0" + date.getDate()).slice(-2));
}
```

Listing 14-5: helpers.js

In the *helpers.js* file, we add the export keyword in front of each function. This means that those functions will be available for import from other JS files in our project.

Indeed, in *logic.js*, we start with importing those functions:

```javascript
import {areDatesEqual, getDateOnlyString, getDateOnly} from './helpers.js';

///////////////////////////////////////////////////
///   Business logic
///////////////////////////////////////////////////

//checks whether a time slot is already occupied
export const slotAlreadyTaken = function (state, date, time) {
  if (state.appointments.get(date.toDateString()) !== undefined
    && state.appointments.get(date.toDateString()).get(time) !== undefined)
    return true;
  else
    return false;
}

//update appointment when user presses save
export const updateAppointment = function (state, newDesc, newDate, newTime) {
  let newAppointments = new Map();
  state.appointments.forEach((value, key) => {
    newAppointments.set(key, new Map());
    state.appointments.get(key).forEach((v, k) => {
      if (!(state.selectedDate.toDateString() == key && state.selectedTime == k)) {
        newAppointments.get(key).set(k, state.appointments.get(key).get(k));
      }
    });
  });

  if (!newAppointments.has(newDate.toDateString())) {
    newAppointments.set(newDate.toDateString(), new Map());
  }
  newAppointments.get(newDate.toDateString()).set(newTime, newDesc);

  let newState = {
    appointments: newAppointments,
    displayedDate: newDate,
    selectedDesc: newDesc,
    selectedDate: newDate,
    selectedTime: newTime,
    selectedVisible: state.selectedVisible
  }

  return newState;
}

export const deleteAppointment = function (state, date, time) {
  let newAppointments = new Map();
  state.appointments.forEach((value, key) => {
    newAppointments.set(key, new Map());
    state.appointments.get(key).forEach((v, k) => {
      if (!(date.toDateString() == key && time == k)) {
        newAppointments.get(key).set(k, state.appointments.get(key).get(k));
      }
    });
  });
```

```javascript
    let newState = {
      appointments: newAppointments,
      displayedDate: state.displayedDate,
      selectedDesc: "",
      selectedDate: state.selectedDate,
      selectedTime: state.selectedTime,
      selectedVisible: state.selectedVisible
    }

    return newState;
}

//called when the user clicks on a time slot
export const selectSlot = function (state, newTime) {
  let newDesc;

  //get appmt description from Map and display it in text box
  let tmp = state.appointments.get(state.displayedDate.toDateString());
  if (tmp !== undefined) {
    if (tmp.get(newTime) !== undefined) {
      newDesc = tmp.get(newTime);
    }
    else {
      newDesc = "";
    }
  }
  else {
    newDesc = "";
  }

  let newState = {
    appointments: state.appointments,
    displayedDate: state.displayedDate,
    selectedDesc: newDesc,
    selectedDate: state.displayedDate,
    selectedTime: newTime,
    selectedVisible: true
  }

  return newState;

}

//update the displayedDate variable
export const updateDisplayedDate = function(state, newDate){
  let newDisplayedDate = getDateOnly(newDate);

  let newState = {
    appointments: state.appointments,
    displayedDate: newDisplayedDate,
    selectedDesc: state.selectedDesc,
    selectedDate: newDisplayedDate,
    selectedTime: state.selectedTime,
```

```
      selectedVisible: false
  }
  return newState;
}

//increase/descrease displayedDate
export const addDaysToDate = function(state, days){
  let newDisplayedDate = state.displayedDate;
  newDisplayedDate.setDate(state.displayedDate.getDate() + days);

  let newState = {
    appointments: state.appointments,
    displayedDate: newDisplayedDate,
    selectedDesc: state.selectedDesc,
    selectedDate: state.selectedDate,
    selectedTime: state.selectedTime,
    selectedVisible: false
  }
  return newState;
}
```

Listing 14-6: logic.js

We also add the export keyword to the logic functions, as they will be used in the *ui.js* file (but also from Jest later on).

Here is the *ui.js* file, with all the imports:

```
import {slotAlreadyTaken, updateAppointment, deleteAppointment,
  selectSlot, updateDisplayedDate, addDaysToDate } from './logic.js';
import {areDatesEqual, getDateOnlyString, getDateOnly} from './helpers.js';

const displayedDateEl = document.getElementById("displayedDate");
const previousDateEl = document.getElementById("previousDate");
const nextDateEl = document.getElementById("nextDate");
const gotoDateEl = document.getElementById("gotoDate");
const appointmentFormEl = document.getElementById("appointmentForm");
const appointmentsListEl = document.getElementById("appointments");
const appointmentDescEl = document.getElementById("appointmentDesc");
const appointmentDateEl = document.getElementById("appointmentDate");
const appointmentTimeEl = document.getElementById("appointmentTime");
const saveEl = document.getElementById("save");
const deleteEl = document.getElementById("delete");


///////////////////////////////////////////////////
///   UI Functions
///////////////////////////////////////////////////

//create initial appointment list
export const createAppointmentList = function () {
  for (let i = 0; i < 24; i++) {
    //create <li> element
    const item = document.createElement("li");
```

```javascript
    const textnode = document.createTextNode(i);
    item.appendChild(textnode);
    item.setAttribute("class", "list-group-item");
    item.setAttribute("id", "hour_" + i);
    item.addEventListener("click", handleClickOnHour);
    appointmentsListEl.appendChild(item);

    //create <option> for hours <select> element
    const option = document.createElement("option");
    const textnode_option = document.createTextNode(i);
    option.setAttribute("value", i);
    option.appendChild(textnode_option);
    appointmentTimeEl.append(option);
  }
}

//clear appointments from list
export const clearAppointmentsList = function () {
  for (let i = 0; i < 24; i++) {
    document.getElementById("hour_" + i).innerHTML = i;
    document.getElementById("hour_" + i).classList.remove("active");
  }
}

//update appointments list
export const updateUI = function (state) {
  displayedDateEl.innerHTML = state.displayedDate.toDateString();
  appointmentDescEl.value = state.selectedDesc;
  appointmentDateEl.value = getDateOnlyString(state.selectedDate);
  appointmentTimeEl.value = state.selectedTime;
  appointmentFormEl.style.visibility  =  (state.selectedVisible)  ?  "visible"  :
"hidden";

  clearAppointmentsList();

  //get appointments for displayed date
  let appointmentsInDay = state.appointments.get(state.displayedDate.toDateString());
  if (appointmentsInDay !== undefined) {
    appointmentsInDay.forEach((value, key) => {
      if (value !== undefined) {
        document.getElementById("hour_" + key).innerHTML = key + "   " + value;
        document.getElementById("hour_" + key).classList.add("active");
      }
    });
  }
  for (let i = 0; i < 24; i++) {
    document.getElementById("hour_" + i)
      .classList.remove("list-group-item-dark");
  }
  document.getElementById("hour_" + state.selectedTime)
    .classList.add("list-group-item-dark");
}

/////////////////////////////////////////////////////
```

```
///  Event handlers
//////////////////////////////////////////////////

//called when user clicks on an hour
const handleClickOnHour = function (event) {
  state = selectSlot(state, event.target.id.substring(5, event.target.id.length));
  updateUI(state);
  appointmentDescEl.focus();
}

//move to next date
const handleNext = function() {
  state = addDaysToDate(state, 1);
  updateUI(state);
}

//move to previous date
const handlePrevious = function() {
  state = addDaysToDate(state, -1);
  updateUI(state);
}

//select new date
const handleGoto = function() {
  let newDateTime = new Date(gotoDateEl.value);
  state = updateDisplayedDate(state, newDateTime);
  updateUI(state);
}

//save/update appointment
const handleSave = function() {
  const newDescr = appointmentDescEl.value;
  const dateTime = new Date(appointmentDateEl.value);
  const newDate = getDateOnly(dateTime);
  const newTime = appointmentTimeEl.value;

  if (slotAlreadyTaken(state, newDate, newTime)
    && !(areDatesEqual(state.selectedDate, newDate)
        && state.selectedTime == newTime)) {
    //ask user to overwrite existing entry
    let ret = confirm("Destination date and time not empty. Overwrite?");
    if (ret) {
      //insert entry to new location
      state = updateAppointment(state, newDescr, newDate, newTime);
      updateUI(state);
    }
  }
  else {
    //insert entry to new location
    state = updateAppointment(state, newDescr, newDate, newTime);
    updateUI(state);
  }
}
```

```javascript
//delete appointment
const handleDelete = function() {
  const dateTime = new Date(appointmentDateEl.value);
  const date = getDateOnly(dateTime);
  const time = parseInt(appointmentTimeEl.value);
  state = deleteAppointment(state, date, time);
  updateUI(state);
}

/////////////////////////////////////////////////////
///  Event listeners
/////////////////////////////////////////////////////

nextDateEl.addEventListener("click", handleNext);
previousDateEl.addEventListener("click", handlePrevious);
gotoDateEl.addEventListener("change", handleGoto);
saveEl.addEventListener("click", handleSave);
deleteEl.addEventListener("click", handleDelete);

/////////////////////////////////////////////////////
///  Startup
/////////////////////////////////////////////////////

let d = new Date();
let state = {
  appointments: new Map(),
  displayedDate: getDateOnly(d),
  selectedDesc: "",
  selectedDate: getDateOnly(d),
  selectedTime: 8,
  selectedVisible: false
};

createAppointmentList();
updateUI(state);
```

Listing 14-7: ui.js

Now we are ready to start the dev server:

```
npm start
```

As a result, the dev server will start, and we will open the web browser to the *index.html* file. Every time we make a change in one of the JS files, then the bundler will run again, it will produce a new *bundle.js* file and will reload automatically the web page.

We can also create the production version of the bundle.js file with the following command:

```
npm build
```

The resulting *bundle.js* file can be found in the *dist* folder.

Now we are ready to use *Jest* to test our code. Jest is mainly used for testing Node.js code. However, Node.js does not have support for ES6 features like import/export, or async/await. Therefore, in order to have our code tested by Jest, we need to transform it into code compatible with Node.js. This is where Babel comes to the rescue.

Babel is a library that is used to transform code written in ES6 into a format that is understood by older browsers or other environments, like Node.js.

We proceed with Babel installation:

```
npm install --save-dev babel-loader @babel/core @babel/preset-env
```

The webpack config file should be updated as follows:

```
const path = require('path');

module.exports = {
  "mode": "none",
  "entry": "./src/ui.js",
  "output": {
    "path": __dirname + '/dist',
    "filename": "bundle.js"
  },
  devServer: {
    contentBase: path.join(__dirname, 'dist')
  },
  "module": {
    "rules": [
      {
        "test": /\.js$/,
        "exclude": /node_modules/,
        "use": {
          "loader": "babel-loader",
          "options": {
            "presets": ["@babel/preset-env",]
          }
        }
      },
    ]
  }
};
```

Listing 14-8: webpack.config.js

We should also create a Babel configuration file (named *.babelrc*) in the root folder:

```
{
  "presets": ["@babel/preset-env"]
}
```

Listing 14-9: .babelrc

Then, we install Jest:

```
npm install jest babel-jest --save-dev
```

We will create a new folder (named *tests*) that will contain all our tests:

```
mkdir tests
```

Inside this folder we will create a file (named *helpers.spec.js*) that will contain the tests for our *helper.js* file:

```
import {areDatesEqual} from '../src/helpers.js';

describe("Helpers testing", () => {
  it("When dates are not equal - areDatesEqual() returns false", () => {
    let d1 = new Date(2023, 12, 31);
    let d2 = new Date(2023, 12, 30);

    expect(areDatesEqual(d1, d2)).toBe(false);
    });

  it("When dates are equal - areDatesEqual() returns true", () => {
    let d1 = new Date(2023, 12, 31);
    let d2 = new Date(2023, 12, 31);

    expect(areDatesEqual(d1, d2)).toBe(true);
    });
});
```

Listing 14-10: helpers.spec.js

We can now run the tests through npm:

```
npm test
```

Here is the result:

```
> appointments@1.0.0 test
> jest

 PASS  tests/helpers.spec.js
  Helpers testing
    √ When dates are not equal - areDatesEqual() returns false (4 ms)
    √ When dates are equal - areDatesEqual() returns true (1 ms)

Test Suites: 1 passed, 1 total
Tests:       2 passed, 2 total
Snapshots:   0 total
Time:        0.941 s, estimated 1 s
Ran all test suites.
```

Let's now migrate the logic test cases from QUnit to Jest. We will use the assertion style that Jest uses, like the following:

- expect(expression).toBe(value)
- expect(*expression*).toEqual(*object*)
- expect(*expression*).toBeTruthy()
- expect(*expression*).toBeFalsy()

and many others

```
import { areDatesEqual, getDateOnly } from '../src/helpers.js';
import {
  slotAlreadyTaken,
  updateAppointment,
  deleteAppointment,
  selectSlot
} from '../src/logic.js';

describe("Logic testing", () => {
  it("When appointment already exists at specific date and time - slotAlreadyTaken()
returns true", () => {
    let d = new Date(2024, 1, 10);
    let map = new Map();
    let day = new Map();
    day.set(10, "test");
    map.set(d.toDateString(), day);
    let state = {
      appointments: map,
      displayedDate: getDateOnly(d),
      selectedDesc: "",
      selectedDate: getDateOnly(d),
      selectedTime: 8,
      selectedVisible: false
    };

    expect(slotAlreadyTaken(state, d, 10)).toBeTruthy();
  });

  it("When appointment does not exist at specific date and time - slotAlreadyTaken()
returns false", () => {
    let d = new Date(2024, 1, 10);
    let map = new Map();
    let day = new Map();
    day.set(10, "test");
    map.set(d.toDateString(), day);
    let state = {
      appointments: map,
      displayedDate: getDateOnly(d),
      selectedDesc: "",
      selectedDate: getDateOnly(d),
      selectedTime: 8,
```

```
      selectedVisible: false
    };

    expect(slotAlreadyTaken(state, d, 9)).toBeFalsy();
  });

  it("When updating existing appointment to a new date - the existing one is
removed'", () => {
    let d = new Date(2024, 1, 10);
    let d2 = new Date(2024, 1, 11);
    let map = new Map();
    let day = new Map();
    day.set(10, "test");
    map.set(d.toDateString(), day);
    let state = {
      appointments: map,
      displayedDate: getDateOnly(d),
      selectedDesc: "",
      selectedDate: getDateOnly(d),
      selectedTime: 10,
      selectedVisible: false
    };

    let newState = updateAppointment(state, "test", d2, 7);
    expect(newState.appointments.get(d2.toDateString()).get(7)).toBe("test");
    expect(newState.appointments.get(d.toDateString()).has(10)).toBeFalsy();
  });

  it("When deleting appointment - the appointment is removed", () => {
    let d = new Date(2024, 1, 10);
    let map = new Map();
    let day = new Map();
    day.set(10, "test");
    map.set(d.toDateString(), day);
    let state = {
      appointments: map,
      displayedDate: getDateOnly(d),
      selectedDesc: "",
      selectedDate: getDateOnly(d),
      selectedTime: 10,
      selectedVisible: false
    };

    let newState = deleteAppointment(state, d, 10);
    expect(newState.appointments.get(d.toDateString()).has(10)).toBeFalsy();
  });

  it("When user clicks on an hour slot - the right panel is updated", () => {
    let d = new Date(2024, 1, 10);
    let map = new Map();
    let day = new Map();
    day.set(10, "test");
    map.set(d.toDateString(), day);
    let state = {
```

```
    appointments: map,
    displayedDate: getDateOnly(d),
    selectedDesc: "",
    selectedDate: getDateOnly(d),
    selectedTime: 8,
    selectedVisible: false
  };

  let newState = selectSlot(state, 10);
  expect(newState.selectedDesc).toBe("test");
  expect(areDatesEqual(newState.selectedDate, getDateOnly(d))).toBeTruthy();
  expect(newState.selectedTime).toBe(10);
});

});
```

Listing 14-11: logic.spec.js

We can now run `npm test` again and see the results:

```
> appointments@1.0.0 test
> jest

 PASS  tests/logic.spec.js
 PASS  tests/helpers.spec.js

Test Suites: 2 passed, 2 total
Tests:       7 passed, 7 total
Snapshots:   0 total
Time:        1.145 s
Ran all test suites.
```

You can find this project in GitHub:

https://github.com/htset/vanilla_javascript_projects/tree/main/appointments4

Note: When you fetch the repository to your workspace, you will have to run `npm install` so that NPM will install all the dependencies to your machine. Such files are not saved by Git as a *.gitignore* file is used.

15. Expense tracker

Let's create an application that will track our expenses per month. The expenses of each month will be displayed in a table. Also, we will create a pie chart that will display the sums of the expenses categories for the selected month.

Budget Tracker

Expense Name:

Amount:

Category:

Date:

Add Expense

Monthly expenses

Display Month: 2024-01

Name	Amount	Category	Date
parking	$4.50	other	2024-01-31
Supermarket	$51.00	groceries	2024-01-31
Total Expenses	**$55.50**		

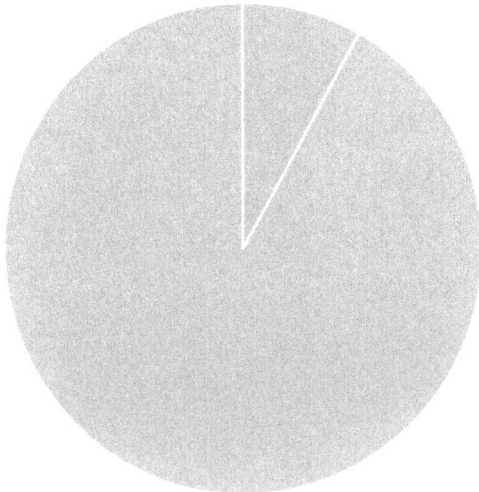

- ES6 classes
- Chart.js
- DOM manipulation
- `map()`, `filter()`, `reduce()` functions

Proposed Solution

This time, we will create the expense tracker by using ES6 classes. We will also separate the JS code into multiple classes and files for better project structure.

First, we will create a new project:

```
npm init
```

Then, we will install Webpack:

```
npm install webpack webpack-cli webpack-dev-server --save-dev
```

and the project dependencies:

```
npm install chart.js moment pikaday
```

Library Chart.js (https://www.chartjs.org) will be used to make the pie chart with the expenses categories. We will use Pikaday (https://github.com/Pikaday/Pikaday) as a date picker. Pikaday also requires the installation of moment.js (https://momentjs.com) for date/time handling.

The package.json file will look like the following:

```
{
  "name": "expense_tracker",
  "version": "1.0.0",
  "description": "",
  "main": "app.js",
  "scripts": {
    "build": "webpack",
    "start": "webpack serve --open",
    "test": "jest"
  },
  "author": "",
  "license": "ISC",
  "devDependencies": {
    "webpack": "^5.90.0",
    "webpack-cli": "^5.1.4",
    "webpack-dev-server": "^4.15.1"
  },
  "dependencies": {
```

```
    "chart.js": "^4.4.1",
    "moment": "^2.30.1",
    "pikaday": "^1.8.2"
  }
}
```
Listing 15-1: package.json

We have added npm scripts to run Webpack's development server and create *bundle.js*.

Here is the *webpack.config.js* file:

```
const path = require('path');

module.exports = {
  "mode": "none",
  "entry": "./src/app.js",
  "output": {
    "path": __dirname + '/dist',
    "filename": "bundle.js"
  },
  "devServer": {
    "static": path.join(__dirname, 'public/'),
    "devMiddleware": {
      "publicPath": '/dist/'
    },
    "port": 3000,
    "hot": "only"
  },
};
```
Listing 15-2: webpack.config.js

Inside the *public* folder, we create the *index.html* file:

```
<!DOCTYPE html>
<html lang="en">

<head>
  <link rel="stylesheet"
    href="https://cdnjs.cloudflare.com/ajax/libs/pikaday/1.8.0/css/pikaday.min.css">
  <link rel="stylesheet" href="styles.css">

  <title>Budget Tracker</title>
</head>

<body>
  <div class="container">
    <h1>Budget Tracker</h1>

    <div id="toastContainer"></div>

    <form id="expenseForm">
      <label for="expenseName">Expense Name:</label>
      <input type="text" id="expenseName" required>
```

```
            <label for="expenseAmount">Amount:</label>
            <input type="number" id="expenseAmount" step=".01" required>

            <label for="expenseCategory">Category:</label>
            <input type="text" id="expenseCategory" required>

            <label for="expenseDate">Date:</label>
            <input type="text" id="expenseDate" required>

            <input type="submit" value="Add Expense" />
        </form>

        <div class="container">

            <h2>Monthly expenses</h2>
            <label for="monthPicker">Display Month:</label>
            <input type="text" id="monthPicker">

            <table id="expenseTable">
                <thead>
                    <tr>
                        <th>Name</th>
                        <th>Amount</th>
                        <th>Category</th>
                        <th>Date</th>
                    </tr>
                </thead>
                <tbody></tbody>
            </table>

            <canvas id="pieChart" width="100" height="100"></canvas>
        </div>
    </div>
    <script src="../dist/bundle.js"></script>
</body>

</html>
```

Listing 15-3: index.html

First, we include a <div> container, that will be used to display messages to the user for a short time (*toast* notifications). Then we add the expense form with the following fields:

- Name
- Amount
- Category
- Date

The amount input field can contain only numbers with up to two decimal points. All of the fields are required.

Next, we have a date picker to select a month. When the selected month changes, the table with the expenses list and the pie chart are reloaded with the data from the specific month.

The list of expenses for the selected month will be displayed into a `<table>` element, while the pie chart will be drawn into a `<canvas>` element.

Let's see the accompanying CSS file:

```css
body {
  font-family: 'Arial', sans-serif;
  margin: 0;
  padding: 0;
  background-color: #f4f4f4;
}

.container {
  max-width: 600px;
  margin: 50px auto;
  background-color: #fff;
  padding: 20px;
  border-radius: 8px;
  box-shadow: 0 0 10px rgba(0, 0, 0, 0.1);
}

h1 {
  text-align: center;
  color: #333;
}

form {
  display: flex;
  flex-direction: column;
  gap: 10px;
}

label {
  font-weight: bold;
}

input {
  padding: 8px;
  border: 1px solid #ccc;
  border-radius: 4px;
}

button {
  padding: 10px;
  background-color: #007bff;
  color: #fff;
  border: none;
  border-radius: 4px;
  cursor: pointer;
}
```

```css
button:hover {
  background-color: #0056b3;
}

table {
  width: 100%;
  margin-top: 20px;
  border-collapse: collapse;
}

table, th, td {
  border: 1px solid #ddd;
}

th, td {
  padding: 10px;
  text-align: left;
}

.total-row {
  background-color: #f0f0f0;
  font-weight: bold;
}

.total-row td {
  padding: 8px;
}

#toastContainer {
  position: fixed;
  top: 16px;
  right: 16px;
  max-width: 300px;
  z-index: 1000;
}

.toast {
  background-color: #333;
  color: #fff;
  padding: 12px;
  margin-bottom: 8px;
  border-radius: 4px;
  box-shadow: 0 4px 8px rgba(0, 0, 0, 0.1);
  transition: opacity 0.3s ease-in-out;
}

.toast:hover {
  opacity: 0.9;
}
```

Listing 15-4: style.css

Note the toastContainer properties: this <div> will be placed at the top right corner of the window, on top of the other elements.

Let's proceed with the JS code. We will use ES6 classes to model the functionality of the expenses, their tracking as well as the handling of the user interface. First, we define a class that will contain the expenses information:

```
export class Expense {
  constructor(name, amount, category, date) {
    this.name = name;
    this.amount = amount;
    this.category = category;
    this.date = date;
  }

  editExpense(newAmount, newCategory, newDate) {
    this.amount = newAmount;
    this.category = newCategory;
    this.date = newDate;
  }
}
```

Listing 15-5: expense.js

Note the export keyword in front of the Expense class; this will make it available for import from the other JS files.

Next, we have a class that will provide the functionality for expense tracking:

```
export class BudgetTracker {
  constructor() {
    this.expensesByMonth = {};
  }

  addExpense(expense) {
    // monthKey form: '2024-01', etc.
    const monthKey = this.getFormattedMonthKey(expense.date);
    if (!this.expensesByMonth[monthKey]) {
      this.expensesByMonth[monthKey] = [];
    }
    this.expensesByMonth[monthKey].push(expense);
  }

  removeExpense(expense) {
    const monthKey = this.getFormattedMonthKey(expense.date);
    if (this.expensesByMonth[monthKey]) {
      const index = this.expensesByMonth[monthKey].indexOf(expense);
      if (index !== -1) {
        this.expensesByMonth[monthKey].splice(index, 1);
      }
    }
  }

  getFormattedMonthKey(date) {
    const year = date.getFullYear();
    const month = date.getMonth() + 1; // Month is zero-based
    return `${year}-${month.toString().padStart(2, '0')}`;
```

```
  }

  getExpensesForMonth(monthKey) {
    return this.expensesByMonth[monthKey] || [];
  }

  calculateTotalBudget(monthKey) {
    const expenses = this.expensesByMonth[monthKey] || [];
    return expenses.reduce((total, expense) => total + expense.amount, 0);
  }
}
```

Listing 15-6: budgetTracker.js

In the class constructor we define the structure that will contain the expense objects. This object will have a formatted date string as property keys. For example, the expenses for January 2024 will be stored in an array that will in turn be stored under property '2014-01'.

The `budgetTracker` class provides functions to insert and delete expenses, as well as retrieve a list of the month's expenses. Moreover, it can calculate the total monthly expenses. This is performed with the `reduce()` function: we loop over the expenses list by adding each time the expense `amount` to the `total` variable.

Note that the two classes that we have seen so far are agnostic of the UI, as they contain only business logic, so they can be tested with ease.

Next, we can examine the UI logic:

```
import { Expense } from './expense.js';
import { Chart } from 'chart.js/auto';

export class BudgetUI {
  static ctx = document.getElementById('pieChart').getContext('2d');
  static categories = [];
  static expenses = [];
  static pieChart = new Chart(this.ctx, {
    type: 'pie',
    data: {
      labels: this.categories,
      datasets: [{
        data: this.expenses,
        backgroundColor: [
          'rgba(255, 99, 132, 0.7)',
          'rgba(54, 162, 235, 0.7)',
          'rgba(255, 206, 86, 0.7)',
          'rgba(75, 192, 192, 0.7)'
        ],
      }],
    },
  });

  static renderExpenseInTable(expense) {
```

```
  const tableBody = document.querySelector('#expenseTable tbody');

  const row = tableBody.insertRow();
  const nameCell = row.insertCell(0);
  const amountCell = row.insertCell(1);
  const categoryCell = row.insertCell(2);
  const dateCell = row.insertCell(3);

  nameCell.textContent = expense.name;
  amountCell.textContent = `$${expense.amount.toFixed(2)}`;
  categoryCell.textContent = expense.category;
  dateCell.textContent = expense.date.toISOString().split('T')[0];
}

static renderTable(budgetTracker, monthKey) {
  // Clear existing table content
  const tableBody = document.querySelector('#expenseTable tbody');
  tableBody.innerHTML = '';

  // Render expenses in the table
  const expensesForMonth = budgetTracker.getExpensesForMonth(monthKey);
  expensesForMonth.forEach((expense) => {
    BudgetUI.renderExpenseInTable(expense);
  });

  // Add a final row with the total expenses for the month
  const totalRow = tableBody.insertRow();
  totalRow.classList.add('total-row');

  const totalLabelCell = totalRow.insertCell(0);
  totalLabelCell.textContent = 'Total Expenses';

  const totalAmountCell = totalRow.insertCell(1);
  totalAmountCell.textContent =
      `$${budgetTracker.calculateTotalBudget(monthKey).toFixed(2)}`;
}

static renderPieChart(budgetTracker, monthKey) {
  this.categories = [];
  // Get expenses for the selected month
  this.expenses = budgetTracker.getExpensesForMonth(monthKey);

  // Get the categories for those expenses
  this.expenses.forEach((expense) => {
    if (!this.categories.includes(expense.category)) {
      this.categories.push(expense.category);
    }
  });

  // Calculate the total expenditure per category
  const data = this.categories
    .map(category =>
      this.expenses
        .filter(expense => expense.category === category)
```

```
        .reduce((total, exp) => total + exp.amount, 0));

    // Update pie with new data
    this.pieChart.data.datasets[0].data = data;
    this.pieChart.update();
}

static changeMonth(budgetTracker) {
    const monthPicker = document.getElementById('monthPicker');
    const selectedMonth = monthPicker.value;
    const expensesForMonth = budgetTracker.getExpensesForMonth(selectedMonth);

    // Render table and chart again
    this.renderTable(budgetTracker, selectedMonth);
    this.renderPieChart(budgetTracker, selectedMonth);
}

static handleUserInput(budgetTracker) {
    const monthPicker = document.getElementById('monthPicker');
    const expenseForm = document.getElementById('expenseForm');

    // Handle submit event
    expenseForm.addEventListener('submit', (event) => {
        event.preventDefault();

        const expenseName = document.getElementById('expenseName').value;
        const expenseAmount=parseFloat(document.getElementById('expenseAmount').value);
        const expenseCategory = document.getElementById('expenseCategory').value;
        const expenseDate = document.getElementById('expenseDate').value;

        if (isNaN(expenseAmount) || expenseAmount <= 0) {
            alert('Please enter a valid amount for the expense.');
            return;
        }

        const newExpense = new Expense(expenseName, expenseAmount,
            expenseCategory, new Date(expenseDate));
        budgetTracker.addExpense(newExpense);

        // Render table and chart again
        this.renderTable(budgetTracker, monthPicker.value);
        this.renderPieChart(budgetTracker, monthPicker.value);

        // Display toast when a new expense is added
        this.showToast(`New expense added: ${newExpense.name}
            ($$${newExpense.amount})`);

        // Reset form
        expenseForm.reset();
    });
}

static showToast(message, duration = 3000) {
    const toastContainer = document.getElementById('toastContainer');
```

```
    const toast = document.createElement('div');
    toast.className = 'toast';
    toast.textContent = message;

    toastContainer.appendChild(toast);

    // Show toast for a specific duration, then hide it
    setTimeout(() => {
      toast.remove();
    }, duration);
  }
}
```
Listing 15-7: budgetUI.js

We use the `BudgetUI` class to group all UI related functions in one place. This class will have only *static* members, functions and variables. In this way, we don't need to use an instance of the class and the functions are called directly using the class name. In any case, it would also be ok to have a regular class.

Inside the class, we define only *static* properties. First, we get the drawing context from the pie chart `<canvas>` element. Next, we define the arrays for monthly expenses and categories. Finally, we define a new chart object: we pass the references to the expenses and categories lists to be used as data and labels in the pie chart respectively.

Function `renderExpenseInTable()` creates a table row and fills it with information about an expense event. This function is used by `renderTable()` to create each row for all monthly expenses. At the end of the table, we add a final row with the monthly budget total.

The `renderPieChart()` function calculates the total expenditure per category:

```
const data = this.categories
  .map(category =>
    this.expenses
      .filter(expense => expense.category === category)
      .reduce((total, exp) => total + exp.amount, 0));
```

This is achieved with a combination of the `map()`, `filter()` and `reduce()` functions. As result we get an array of the total expenses per category. We use this array to update the pie chart.

The `changeMonth()` function is called when the user selects a new month value with the month picker. The respective expenses for the specific month are retrieved and are used to update the table and the pie chart.

Function `handleUserInput()` handles the submit event from the expense form. It adds the new expense into the budget tracker and triggers the update of the table and the chart.

The `showToast()` function creates a toast notification and displays it at the top right of the screen. A timer is set to hide the notification after some time.

Finally, let's see the entry point, the app.js file:

```javascript
import { BudgetUI } from './budgetUI.js';
import { BudgetTracker } from './budgetTracker.js';
import Pikaday from 'pikaday';
import moment from 'moment';

document.addEventListener('DOMContentLoaded', function () {
  const expenseDateInput = document.getElementById('expenseDate');
  const pikaday = new Pikaday({
    field: expenseDateInput,
    format: 'YYYY-MM-DD',
    defaultDate: moment().toDate(),//current date
    setDefaultDate: true,
  });

  const monthPickerInput = document.getElementById('monthPicker');
  const pikadayMonthPicker = new Pikaday({
    field: monthPickerInput,
    format: 'YYYY-MM',
    defaultDate: moment().toDate(), //current date
    setDefaultDate: true,
    yearRange: [2024, new Date().getFullYear()],
    showYearDropdown: true,
    onSelect: function () {
      BudgetUI.changeMonth(budgetTracker);
    },
  });
});

const budgetTracker = new BudgetTracker();
BudgetUI.handleUserInput(budgetTracker);
BudgetUI.changeMonth(budgetTracker);
```

Listing 15-8: app.js

Here we define two Pikaday objects for the two date pickers of the user interface. In the second one we register a handler for the `select` event: `changeMonth()` will be called when the user selects a new month.

Finally, we create an instance of the `BudgetTracker` class and we call `handleUserInput()` and `changeMonth()` for the first time.

You can find this project in GitHub:

https://github.com/htset/vanilla_javascript_projects/tree/main/expense_tracker

16. Currencies portfolio

We will create a currencies portfolio, where we can report the amounts of various currencies that we have in our possession. Our web app will use `fetch()` to retrieve the latest currency values from a web API and will calculate the total value of the portfolio in the preferred currency.

Concepts covered

`fetch()`

- Asynchronous programming (`async`/`await`, promises)
- DOM manipulation (`querySelector`)

Proposed Solution

For the retrieval of the currency quotes we will the Free Currency API web site (https://freecurrencyapi.com/) that provides a free service for limited API requests. You will have to sign up and get your own API Key to use in your RESTful requests.

There are two types of API requests that we will use:

To get the supported currencies:

```
https://api.freecurrencyapi.com/v1/currencies?apikey=XXXX
```

To get the currency quotes:

```
https://api.freecurrencyapi.com/v1/latest?base_currency=baseCurrency&apikey=XXXX
```

In both cases, we need to supply our API key, while on the latter case we must also provide the three-letter code for the base currency (i.e.: EUR, USD, etc.).

Let's start with the *index.html* file:

```
<!DOCTYPE html>
<html>

<head>
  <title>My Portfolio</title>
  <link
  href="https://cdn.jsdelivr.net/npm/bootstrap@5.2.3/dist/css/bootstrap.min.css"
  rel="stylesheet"
  integrity="sha384-rbsA2VBKQhggwzxH7pPCaAqO46MgnOM80zW1RWuH61DGLwZJEdK2Kadq2F9CUG65"
  crossorigin="anonymous">
</head>

<body>
  <div class="container">
    <h1>My portfolio</h1>

    <div class="row border bg-secondary">
      <div class="col-md-2 m-2">
        <span>Base currency:</span>
      </div>
      <div class="col-md-4 m-2">
        <select class="baseCurrency"></select>
      </div>
    </div>

    <div class="row">
      <div class="col-md-2 m-2">
        <div class="fw-bold">Amount</div>
      </div>
      <div class="col-md-4 m-2">
        <span class="fw-bold">Currency</span>
      </div>
      <div class="col-md-2 m-2">
        <button class="add col-md-12">Add line</button>
      </div>
    </div>

    <div class="list"></div>

    <div class="row border bg-secondary">
      <div class="col-md-2 m-2">
        <button class="calculate col-md-12">Calculate portfolio value</button>
      </div>
      <div class="col-md-4 m-2">
        <div class="result"></div>
      </div>
    </div>
  </div>
  <script
  src="https://cdn.jsdelivr.net/npm/bootstrap@5.2.3/dist/js/bootstrap.bundle.min.js"
  integrity="sha384-kenU1KFdBIe4zVF0s0G1M5b4hcpxyD9F7jL+jjXkk+Q2h455rYXK/7HAuoJl+0I4"
  crossorigin="anonymous"></script>
  <script src="script.js" type="text/javascript"></script>
</body>
```

```
</html>
```
Listing 16-1: index.html

Our HTML file uses Bootstrap for styling; we don't use a separate CSS file.

Let's move on to the JavaScript code. First, we define our element variables and then retrieve the supported currencies from the web service:

```javascript
const baseCurrencyEl = document.querySelector(".baseCurrency");
const currenciesEl = document.querySelector('.list');
const addEl = document.querySelector(".add");
const calculateEl = document.querySelector(".calculate");
const resultEl = document.querySelector(".result");

const fetchSupportedCurrencies = async () => {
  const URL = `https://api.freecurrencyapi.com/v1/currencies?apikey=XXX`;
  let json;
  try {
    const response = await fetch(URL);
    json = await response.json();
    if (!response.ok) {
      alert(`Error ${response.status}: ${json.message}`);
      return null;
    }
    if (json.error !== undefined) {
      alert(`Error: ${json.error.info}`);
      return null;
    }
  }
  catch (error) {
    if (error instanceof SyntaxError) {
      alert("The returned data was invalid");
      return null;
    }
    else {
      alert("There was an error with the request");
      return null;
    }
  }
  return json;
}
```
Listing 16-2: script.js

Function `fetchSupportedCurrencies()` is an `async` function: that's because inside the function we use `await` to call `fetch()` asynchronously.

We first use `fetch()` to get the response. The `response` object is a *Promise*; therefore, we should `await` on it to complete. When the request is complete, we await one more time to get the JSON content of the returned response. We check the response status to see if it was successful and, in this case, we return the parsed JSON object.

Note that we are using a try/catch exception clause to check for the cases where the data returned is invalid or where there was an error with the request.

In the same manner, we send a RESTful GET request to the API, to retrieve the quotes for a selected currency:

```js
const fetchQuotes = async (baseCurrency) => {
  const URL =
`https://api.freecurrencyapi.com/v1/latest?base_currency=${baseCurrency}&apikey=XXX`;
  let json;
  try {
    const response = await fetch(URL);
    json = await response.json();
    if (!response.ok) {
      alert(`Error ${response.status}: ${json.message}`);
      return null;
    }
    if (json.error !== undefined) {
      alert(`Error: ${json.error.info}`);
      return null;
    }
  }
  catch (error) {
    if (error instanceof SyntaxError) {
      alert("The returned data was invalid");
      return null;
    }
    else {
      alert("There was an error with the request");
      return null;
    }
  }
  return json;
}
```

Listing 16-3: script.js

Note that we use a string template to create the URL. The *string template* uses back quotes (``) to mark the start and the end of the string. Inside the string we can use the expression ${ } to interpolate the value of a variable.

When the page loads, function `loadSupportedCurrencies()` is called:

```js
const loadSupportedCurrencies = async () => {
  const response = await fetchSupportedCurrencies();
  if (response !== null) {
    supportedCurencies = response.data;

    Object.keys(supportedCurencies).forEach((key) => {
      let option = document.createElement("option");
      option.value = key;
      option.innerHTML = key + "-" + supportedCurencies[key].name;
      baseCurrencyEl.appendChild(option);
```

```
    });
  }
  else {
    supportedCurencies = null;
  }
}
```

Listing 16-4: script.js

This function is also async because it awaits on the async function `fetchSupportedCurrencies()`. This function gets the supported currencies in the form of a JSON object and loops over its contents. In each pass, it creates a new `<option>` element and appends it inside the `<select>` element at the top of the page.

When the *Add Line* button is pressed, the respective handler function is called:

```
const addLine = () => {
  if (supportedCurencies !== null) {
    let rowEl = document.createElement("div");
    rowEl.classList.add("row");
    rowEl.classList.add("border");
    rowEl.classList.add("bg-light");
    rowEl.classList.add("currency-row");

    let divEl1 = document.createElement("div");
    divEl1.classList.add("col-md-2");
    divEl1.classList.add("m-2");
    let inputEl = document.createElement("input");
    inputEl.type = "text";
    inputEl.classList.add("col-md-12");
    divEl1.appendChild(inputEl);

    let divEl2 = document.createElement("div");
    divEl2.classList.add("col-md-4");
    divEl2.classList.add("m-2");
    let selectEl = document.createElement("select");
    selectEl.classList.add("col-md-12");
    Object.keys(supportedCurencies).forEach((key) => {
      let option = document.createElement("option");
      option.value = key;
      option.innerHTML = key + "-" + supportedCurencies[key].name;
      selectEl.appendChild(option);
    });
    divEl2.appendChild(selectEl);

    let divEl3 = document.createElement("div");
    divEl3.classList.add("col-md-2");
    divEl3.classList.add("m-2");
    let deleteEl = document.createElement("button");
    deleteEl.innerHTML = "Remove";
    deleteEl.addEventListener("click", (e) => {
      e.target.parentElement.parentElement.remove();
    });
    deleteEl.classList.add("col-md-12");
```

```
    divEl3.appendChild(deleteEl);

    rowEl.appendChild(divEl1);
    rowEl.appendChild(divEl2);
    rowEl.appendChild(divEl3);

    currenciesEl.appendChild(rowEl);
  }
}
```

Listing 16-5: script.js

This function creates a new <div> that will be placed in the list of the portfolio currencies. It then creates an <input> of type text, a <select> element, and a <button>, that are all placed inside the aforementioned <div>. The <select> element is filled with the supported currencies <option> elements, while the button adds an event listener for the deletion of the row. The handler function is defined inline:

```
deleteEl.addEventListener("click", (e) => {
  e.target.parentElement.parentElement.remove();
});
```

We get the parent element (the <div> containing the specific line) of the parent element (the <div> containing the button) of the button and we remove it from the DOM.

Next, we have the functions that calculate the portfolio:

```
const calculate = (num, selectedCurrency, baseCurrency, quotes) => {
  if (selectedCurrency !== baseCurrency) {
    const rate = quotes.data[selectedCurrency]
    return num / rate;
  }
  return num;
}

Number.prototype.round = function (places) {
  return +(Math.round(this + "e+" + places) + "e-" + places);
}

const calculatePortfolio = () => {
  if (supportedCurencies !== null) {
    //first get updated currency quotes
    const baseCurrency = baseCurrencyEl.value;
    fetchQuotes(baseCurrency)
      .then((quotes) => {
        if (quotes !== null) {
          const portfolioItemsEl = document.querySelectorAll(".currency-row");
          let total = 0;
          portfolioItemsEl.forEach((item) => {
            const amount = item.querySelector("input[type=text]").value;
            const selectedCurrency
              = item.querySelectorAll('option:checked')[0].value
```

```
        let num = parseFloat(amount);
        if (!isNaN(num)) {
          let calculatedAmount
            = calculate(num, selectedCurrency, baseCurrency, quotes);
          total += calculatedAmount.round(2);
        }
      });
      resultEl.innerHTML = total + " " + baseCurrency;
    }
  });
  }
}
```

The `calculatePortfolio()` function is called when the respective button is clicked. First it gets the updated currency quotes for the selected base currency. Note the use of Promises here (the `then()` function), since function `fetchQuotes()` is asynchronous.

Inside the `then()` function of the Promise, i.e. when the Promise is resolved, we add the code that will get all the rows of our portfolio and perform the calculations.

Note that in this project we are using an alternative way to get the references to the DOM elements:

- `document.querySelector()`
- `document.querySelectorAll()`

In both functions we can use a variety of CSS selectors to get the object(s) we want. For example:

```
const amount = item.querySelector("input[type=text]").value
```

Here, we search inside a portfolio row to get the input element of type `text`, which contains the amount of the specific currency.

In our code, we can use both types of functions, either `querySelector`/`querySelectorAll`, or `getElementById`/`getElementsByClassName` etc.; it depends on the occasion. In general, it is better to use `getElementById` when we use an ID, and `querySelector`/`All` when using a class name.

One significant difference between the two families is that `querySelectorAll` gives us a static node list while `getElementsByClassName` gives us a live node list, that gets updated when we add/remove elements from it.

One last note: we create a function `round()` in the Number object prototype, that will round the numbers correctly to a specific number of decimal places.

Finally, here is the startup code:

```javascript
calculateEl.addEventListener("click", calculatePortfolio)
addEl.addEventListener("click", addLine);
let supportedCurencies;

loadSupportedCurrencies()
  .then(() => {
    addLine();
  });
```

Listing 16-7: script.js

You can find this project in GitHub:

https://github.com/htset/vanilla_javascript_projects/tree/main/currencies

17. OpenLayer maps with meteo information

In this project, we will create an OpenLayers web application that will present temperature information. When the user presses on the map, a pop-up will appear indicating the temperature in the specific location. Moreover, when the application is loaded, it will center and zoom on to the user's location and will also show the current temperature there.

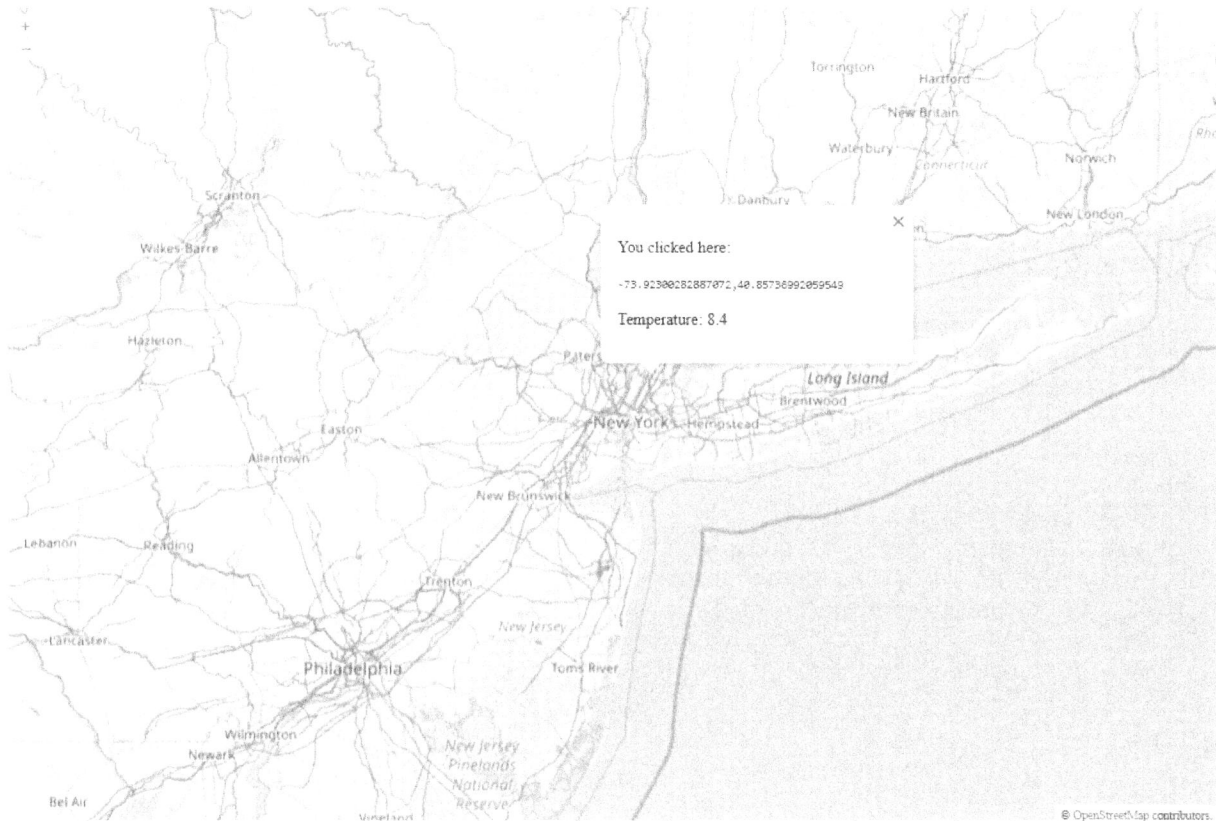

Concepts covered

- Map handling
- Geolocation
- API requests

Proposed Solution

Google Maps would be the obvious option here, but to get an API key, lately we need to provide credit card information. For this reason, we will opt to use OpenLayers (https://openlayers.org) which is a service that provides a free API.

Although we can link to the OpenLayers library directly in our HTML file, we will use a package manager, Vite (https://vitejs.dev), a more recent option compared to Webpack.

We will create a new project by typing in a command prompt:

```
npx create-ol-app meteo --template vite
```

This creates a *package.json* project file and downloads the required files. It also creates a very simple Vite configuration file:

```
export default {
  build: {
    sourcemap: true,
  }
}
```

Listing 17-1: vite.config.js

Here is our HTML file:

```
<!DOCTYPE html>
<html lang="en">
  <head>
    <meta charset="UTF-8" />
    <link rel="icon" type="image/x-icon" href="https://openlayers.org/favicon.ico" />
    <meta name="viewport" content="width=device-width, initial-scale=1.0" />
    <title>Meteo with OpenLayers</title>
  </head>
  <body>
    <div id="map"></div>
    <div id="popup" class="ol-popup">
      <a href="#" id="popup-close" class="ol-popup-close"></a>
      <div id="popup-content"></div>
    </div>
    <script type="module" src="./main.js"></script>
  </body>
</html>
```

Listing 17-2:index.html

There are two main <div> elements in our HTML. The first one is where the map is going to appear. The second one is the popup that will display the temperature value.

The CSS file is as follows:

```
@import "node_modules/ol/ol.css";

html, body {
  margin: 0;
  height: 100%;
}

#map {
  position: absolute;
  top: 0;
  bottom: 0;
  width: 100%;
}
```

```css
.ol-popup {
  position: absolute;
  background-color: white;
  box-shadow: 0 1px 4px rgba(0,0,0,0.2);
  padding: 15px;
  border-radius: 10px;
  border: 1px solid #cccccc;
  bottom: 12px;
  left: -50px;
  min-width: 280px;
}

.ol-popup:after, .ol-popup:before {
  top: 100%;
  border: solid transparent;
  content: " ";
  height: 0;
  width: 0;
  position: absolute;
  pointer-events: none;
}

.ol-popup:after {
  border-top-color: white;
  border-width: 10px;
  left: 48px;
  margin-left: -10px;
}

.ol-popup:before {
  border-top-color: #cccccc;
  border-width: 11px;
  left: 48px;
  margin-left: -11px;
}

.ol-popup-close {
  text-decoration: none;
  position: absolute;
  top: 2px;
  right: 8px;
}

.ol-popup-close:after {
  content: "✖";
}
```

Listing 17-3: script.js

Most of the CSS code deals with the styling of the popup. We use *absolute positioning* for the map and the popup. Note also, that we import the corresponding CSS files from the Open Layers library at the top of the page.

Now, let's examine the JS code. The temperature information is retrieved from Open Meteo (https://open-meteo.com), a free meteo API service. Here, we don't have to get an API key; we can send GET requests directly to this URL:

```
https://api.open-meteo.com/v1/forecast?latitude=X&longitude=X&current=temperature_2m
```

We provide the latitude and the longitude values of the location, and we send a request for the temperature at 2 meters from the ground (there are also many variables that we can get from this API).

At the beginning of the JS file, we import the OpenLayer classes, and we get the references of the elements:

```
import './style.css';
import { Map, View } from 'ol';
import TileLayer from 'ol/layer/Tile';
import OSM from 'ol/source/OSM';
import VectorSource from 'ol/source/Vector.js';
import VectorLayer from 'ol/layer/Vector.js';
import Feature from 'ol/Feature';
import Point from 'ol/geom/Point';
import { toLonLat, fromLonLat } from 'ol/proj';
import Overlay from 'ol/Overlay';

const container = document.getElementById('popup');
const content = document.getElementById('popup-content');
const close = document.getElementById('popup-close');
```

Listing 17-4: main.js

Note that we can import the CSS stylesheet from the JS code.

Next, we define the async function that will fetch the temperature data from the API:

```
const getTemp = async function(lat, lon) {
  try {
    const URL = 'https://api.open-meteo.com/v1/forecast?latitude='
      + lat + '&longitude=' + lon + '&current=temperature_2m';
    const response = await fetch(URL);
    if (!response.ok) {
      throw new Error("Error in network response");
    }
    const temp = await response.json();
    return temp.current.temperature_2m;
  }
  catch (error) {
    console.error("There has been a problem with fetch:", error);
    return null;
  }
}
```

Listing 17-5: main.js

Then, we define the async function that will be called when the user clicks on the map:

```
//show popup on map
const handleClickOnMap = async function(event) {
  var point = map.getCoordinateFromPixel(event.pixel);
  var lonLat = toLonLat(point);

  let temp = await getTemp(lonLat[1], lonLat[0]);
  if (temp !== null) {
    content.innerHTML
      = '<p>You clicked here:</p><code>' + lonLat
        + '</code><p>Temperature: ' + temp + '</p>';
  }
  else {
    content.innerHTML
      = '<p>You clicked here:</p><code>' + lonLat
      + '</code><p>There was an error with the request</p>';
  }
  overlay.setPosition(point);
}
```

Listing 17-6: main.js

We get the coordinates from the pixel on the map, and we translate them into longitude and latitude values. We use those values to get the temperature at the specific location. We then formulate the popup message, and we display it on the map.

Next, we define the Open Layers object that we will use in our application. We define a Map object that corresponds to the actual map shown. We also define a View object that will be used to center the map and set the zoom level. We also define an Overlay object that will contain the popup:

```
//An overlay to anchor the popup to the map.
const overlay = new Overlay({
  element: container,
  autoPan: {
    animation: {
      duration: 250,
    },
  },
});

//The view object
const view = new View({
  center: [0, 0],
  zoom: 1,
});

//The map object
```

```
const map = new Map({
  target: 'map',
  layers: [
    new TileLayer({
      source: new OSM()
    })
  ],
  overlays: [overlay],
  view: view
});
```

Listing 17-7: main.js

Now, we will define the callback function that will be called when our application gets geolocation information from the browser. The users will be asked to allow access to their location. If permission is granted, then this function will be called:

```
//If we have geolocation --> we center the map to our location
// and we display the current temperature
const centerToPosition = async function(position) {

  //add marker on user's location
  var layer = new VectorLayer({
    source: new VectorSource({
      features: [
        new Feature({
          geometry: new Point(fromLonLat(
            [
              position.coords.longitude,
              position.coords.latitude
            ]))
        })
      ]
    })
  });
  map.addLayer(layer);

  //get temperature for user's location
  let temp = await getTemp(position.coords.latitude,
    position.coords.longitude);
  if (temp !== null) {
    content.innerHTML
      = '<p>Temperature: ' + temp + '</p>';
  }
  else {
    content.innerHTML
      = '<p>There was an error with the request</p>';
  }

  //set position of the popup on user's location
  var point = fromLonLat([position.coords.longitude,
    position.coords.latitude]);
  overlay.setPosition(point);
```

```
  //create a new View object with new coordinates
  // and zoom level
  const newView = new View({
    center: fromLonLat(
      [
        position.coords.longitude,
        position.coords.latitude
      ]),
    zoom: 10,
  });

  //update map to new View
  map.setView(newView);
}
```

Listing 17-8: main.js

First, we create a new VectorLayer object that will be used to place a marker of the user's location on the map. Then, we get the temperature for the user's location, and we formulate the text for the popup. We use the Overlay object to display the popup on the map. We also create a new View object with a new center (the user's location) and a higher zoom level. We set the map's view to our new View object. As a result, the map will center and zoom on to the user's location.

Finally, we define the event listeners for the map and the popup. We also add the startup code:

```
//When we click on the map
map.on('click', handleClickOnMap);

//When the popup should be closed
close.onclick = function () {
  overlay.setPosition(undefined);
  close.blur();
  return false;
};

//Startup: we ask the user if geolocation is allowed
if (navigator.geolocation) {
  navigator.geolocation.getCurrentPosition(centerToPosition);
}
```

Listing 17-9: main.js

You can find this project in GitHub:

https://github.com/htset/vanilla_javascript_projects/tree/main/meteo

18. Product list with infinite scroll

Let's create a web page that will load products from an API service. The products will be fetched and displayed on the web page in batches.

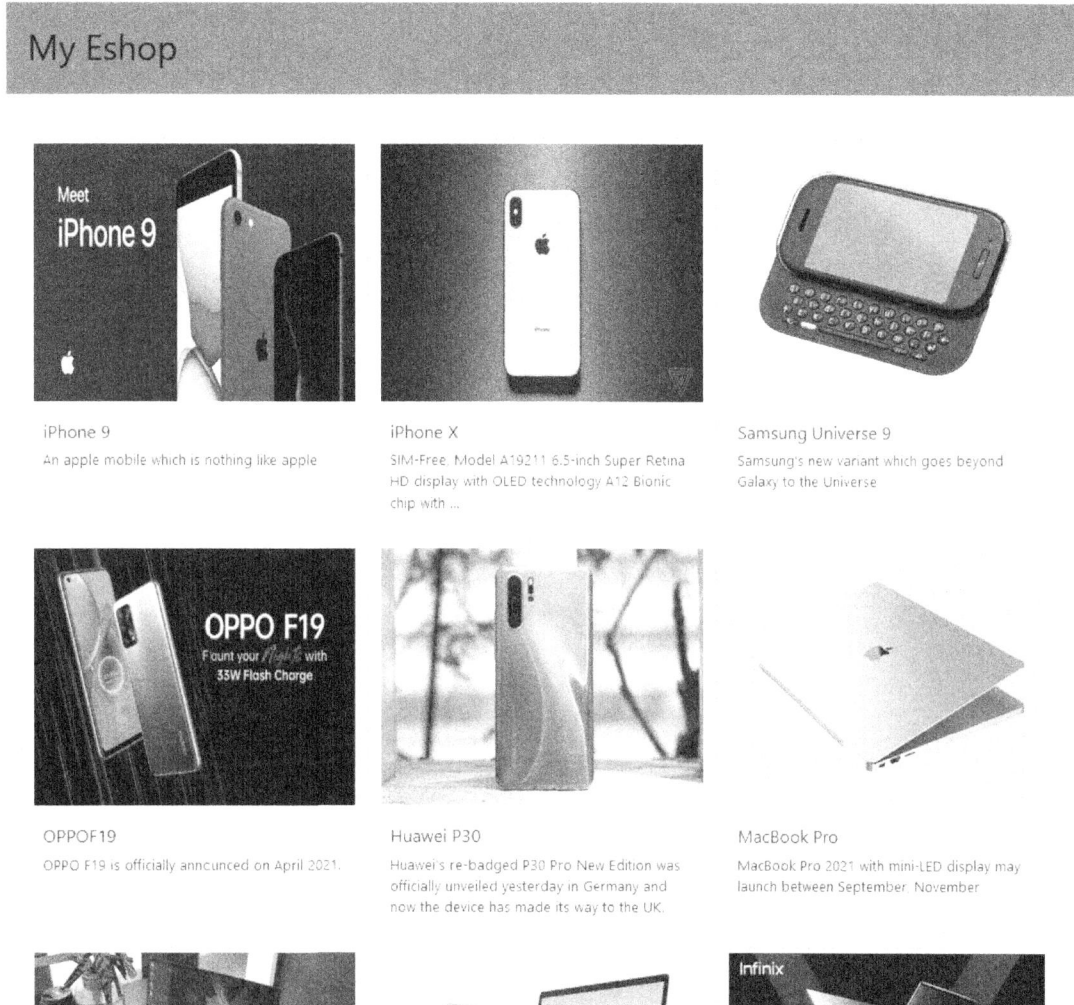

Concepts covered

- Pagination
- Infinite scroll
- Timers

Proposed Solution

In order to test our application, we can use a dummy API service to retrieve information and images of products in JSON. More specifically, we will use DummyJSON (https://dummyjson.com), which is a free service with various interesting resources.

Let's view the HTML file:

```
<!DOCTYPE html>
<html lang="en">

<head>
  <title>My Eshop</title>
  <link
  href="https://cdn.jsdelivr.net/npm/bootstrap@5.2.3/dist/css/bootstrap.min.css"
  rel="stylesheet"
  integrity="sha384-rbsA2VBKQhggwzxH7pPCaAqO46MgnOM80zW1RWuH61DGLwZJEdK2Kadq2F9CUG65"
  crossorigin="anonymous">
</head>

<body>
  <div class="container">
    <header class="bg-primary text-black p-4 m-4">
      <h1>My Eshop</h1>
    </header>

    <div class="d-flex justify-content-center m-5">
      <div class="products row row-cols-3 g-3"></div>
    </div>

    <div class="d-flex justify-content-center m-5">
      <div class="spinner-border" role="status">
      </div>
    </div>

  </div>
  <script
  src="https://cdn.jsdelivr.net/npm/bootstrap@5.2.3/dist/js/bootstrap.bundle.min.js"
  integrity="sha384-kenU1KFdBIe4zVF0s0G1M5b4hcpxyD9F7jL+jjXkk+Q2h455rYXK/7HAuoJl+0I4"
  crossorigin="anonymous"></script>
  <script src="script.js" type="text/javascript"></script>
</body>

</html>
```

Listing 18-1:index.html

There are two main `<div>` elements in our HTML. The first one is where the product list is going to appear (class `products`). The second one is the spinner that will be displayed during product loading (class `spinner-border`). We use *Bootstrap* styling, so we will not include our own CSS file.

The JS code begins with getting the main elements' references and defining the function to fetch data from the API service:

```
const productsEl = document.querySelector('.products');
const spinnerEl = document.querySelector('.spinner-border');

const fetchProducts = async (limit, skip) => {
  const URL = `https://dummyjson.com/products/?limit=${limit}&skip=${skip}`;
  const response = await fetch(URL);
```

```
  if (!response.ok) {
    throw new Error(`Error: ${response.status}`);
  }
  return await response.json();
}
```

Listing 18-2: script.js

This is an async function as it has to await on the fetch() operation. Our function has two parameters that will enable pagination:

- limit: how many items will be fetched
- skip: how many items will be skipped from the start

For instance, with limit=10 and skip=50 we will fetch 10 items starting from the 51st item in the line of products.

Next, we define the function that will render the product information on the page:

```
const renderProducts = (products) => {
  products.forEach(product => {
    const productEl = document.createElement('div');
    productEl.classList.add('card');
    productEl.style = "width: 25rem;"

    productEl.innerHTML = `
      <img src="${product.thumbnail}"
        class="card-img-top img-thumbnail" style="height:300px">
        <div class="card-body">
        <h5 class="card-title">${product.title}</h5>
        <p class="card-text">${product.description}</p>`;

    productsEl.appendChild(productEl);
  });
};
```

Listing 18-3: script.js

For each product in the returned JSON array, we create a new <div> element, that has the Bootstrap card style class. Inside the card, we place the thumbnail image, the title, and the description of the product. The image is loaded directly from the DummyJSON server; we just enter its URL that is provided by the API. Finally, the new <div> element is appended to the products list <div> element.

Next, we create the async function the will call the former two functions, but only when there are any more products to fetch:

```
const loadProducts = async (page, limit) => {
  showSpinner();
  try {
    if (skip < total || total == 0) {
      const response = await fetchProducts(page, limit);
```

```
      renderProducts(response.products);
      total = response.total;
    }
  }
  catch (error) {
    console.log(error.message);
  }
  hideSpinner();
};

const hideSpinner = () => {
  spinnerEl.style.visibility = "hidden";
};

const showSpinner = () => {
  spinnerEl.style.visibility = "visible";
};
```

Listing 18-4: script.js

The response from the Web API contains the total parameter, with the total amount of products available. We will save this value in our local total variable and will compare it with the skip parameter, to understand whether there are any products left to fetch. This function shows the spinner <div> at the beginning of the fetch operation and hides it when the response has been displayed in the web page.

Next, we have the handleScroll() function that is called when the scroll event is emitted:

```
const handleScroll = () => {
  if (timerRunning)
    return;
  timerRunning = true;

  setTimeout(() => {
    const docEl = document.documentElement;

    if (docEl.scrollTop + docEl.clientHeight >= docEl.scrollHeight - 10) {
      skip += limit;
      loadProducts(limit, skip);
    }
    timerRunning = false;
  }, 1000);
};

window.addEventListener('scroll', handleScroll);
```

Listing 18-5: script.js

The scroll event is called many times as we are scrolling our page. To avoid calling the loadProducts() function too many times, we will add a delay of one second, with the use of the setTimeout() function. When the callback function is run, it will use the scrollTop, clientHeight and scrollHeight properties to figure out whether it should fetch the next batch of products. We use the `timerRunning` boolean value to control whether `setTimeout()` will be called or skipped.

Finally, we initialize the parameters used and we load the first batch of the products in the list:

```
const limit = 12;
let total = 0;
let skip = 0;
var timerRunning;

loadProducts(limit, skip);
```

Listing 18-6: script.js

You can find this project in GitHub:

https://github.com/htset/vanilla_javascript_projects/tree/main/scroll

19. Netflix clone

In this project, we will try to emulate the user interface of Netflix (https://www.netflix.com). More specifically, we will create rows of movie icons that can be scrolled left or right. Also, when the mouse hovers over an icon, the movie decription will pop up in a smooth manner.

Concepts covered

- CSS transitions and transformations
- DOM manipulation

Proposed Solution

We will use The MovieDB (https://www.themoviedb.org) free service to get the posters and the titles of the movies. After we become members of the service, we can get an API key for the RESTful requests.

Here is the HTML file of our web page:

```
<!DOCTYPE html>
<html>

<head>
  <title>My Movies</title>
  <link href="style.css" rel="stylesheet">
</head>

<body>
  <img src="logo.png" class="logo" />
  <h2>Trending now</h2>
```

```html
<div class="container">
  <div class="previous">
    <i class="fa-solid fa-chevron-left"></i>
  </div>

  <div class="slider">

  </div>

  <div class="next">
    <i class="fa-solid fa-chevron-right"></i>
  </div>

</div>
<h2>Top rated</h2>
<div class="container">
  <div class="previous2">
    <i class="fa-solid fa-chevron-left"></i>
  </div>

  <div class="slider2">

  </div>

  <div class="next2">
    <i class="fa-solid fa-chevron-right"></i>
  </div>

</div>

<script
  src="https://kit.fontawesome.com/cc55d42b25.js"
  crossorigin="anonymous"></script>
<script src="script.js" type="text/javascript"></script>
</body>

</html>
```

Listing 19-1:index.html

Our HTML code features two containers, one for the currently trending movies and one for the top-rated ones. Each container has 3 <div> elements: the previous and next arrows, as well as a slider <div>.

We create the two arrows using the *Font Awsome* (https://fontawesome.com) icon library. We load the JS file for the library at the bottom of the page.

The slider is initially empty and will be filled by using JavaScript.

Let's see now the CSS script:

```css
:root {
  --icon-width: 250px;
  --icon-height: 200px;
```

```css
    --arrow-width: 50px;
}

body{
  background-color: black;
  color:white;
  overflow: hidden; /* Hide scrollbars */
}

.logo{
  width: 200px;
  padding:20px;
}

.container{
  position:relative;
}

.slider, .slider2 {
  white-space: nowrap;
  transition: all 1.0s ease-in-out;
}

.item {
  width: var(--icon-width);
  height: var(--icon-height);
  display: inline-block;
  position: relative;
  color: white;
  font-size: 0.8rem;
  transition: all 0.6s ease-in-out;
  text-align: center;
}

.item:nth-of-type(1) {
  margin-left: var(--arrow-width);
}

.item:hover {
  transform: scale(1.4);
  z-index: 50;
  border: 1px white solid;
  background-color: darkgray;

}

.item:hover > .description {
  visibility:visible;
}

.description{
  width: var(--icon-width);
  white-space: pre-line;
  visibility:hidden;
```

```css
}

.descr-text{
  height: 40px;
  display:block;
  overflow: hidden;
  padding: 0 10px;
  text-align: left;
}

.descr-buttons-container {
  display: flex;
  flex-direction: row;
  padding: 0 10px;

}

.descr-button {
  display: flex;
  align-items: center;
  justify-content: center;
  width: 20px;
  height: 20px;
  border: 2px solid white;
  text-align: center;
  font-size: 8px;
  margin-right: 5px;
  border-radius: 100%;
}

img {
  width: 15rem;
}

.previous,.previous2,
.next, .next2 {
  width: var(--arrow-width);
  height: var(--icon-height);
  border-radius: 5px;
  position: absolute;
  top: 50%;
  background-color: rgba(0, 0, 0, 0.3);
  outline: none;
  border: none;
  color: white;
  z-index: 100;
  cursor: pointer;

}

.next, .next2 {
  right: 0;
}
```

Listing 19-2: style.css

This project is CSS intensive, so we will break the stylesheet in details to explain.

First of all, we use the :root pseudo-class that matches the <html> element. We define here some *CSS variables* that will be used in the following elements:

```
:root {
  --icon-width: 250px;
  --icon-height: 200px;
  --arrow-width: 50px;
}
```

In the body, we use the overflow property to hide the scrollbars that will certainly appear (especially the horizontal one) as the content exceeds the window width:

```
body{
  background-color: black;
  color:white;
  overflow: hidden; /* Hide scrollbars */
}
```

The container <div> gets *relative positioning*. This will be combined with the *absolute positioning* of the arrows, to place them at the edges of their respective container:

```
.container{
  position:relative;
}
```

For the two sliders, we specify a *transition* of one second. This means that the slider movement to the left or the fight will be performed smoothly. The white-space property is used to avoid wrapping of the images on a new line, but instead to be positioned one after the other:

```
.slider, .slider2 {
  white-space: nowrap;
  transition: all 1.0s ease-in-out;
}
```

In the CSS for the item element (i.e. the movie icon) we get the width and the height from the variables defined above. We also set the display property to inline-block: this will make the icons line up. Here again, we define a transition; this will apply during the appearance of the movie description:

```
.item {
  width: var(--icon-width);
  height: var(--icon-height);
  display: inline-block;
```

143

```
  position: relative;
  color: white;
  font-size: 0.8rem;
  transition: all 0.6s ease-in-out;
  text-align: center;
}
```

Next, we define some *pseudo-classes* on the item class. The nth-of-type(1) pseudo-class applies to the first item in the list, i.e. the first icon on the left. This is used to give an extra margin to the left of the slider.

When the mouse pointer hovers over an item, a transformation is applied, and the item becomes 40% bigger. Moreover, the description become visible:

```
.item:nth-of-type(1) {
  margin-left: var(--arrow-width);
}

.item:hover {
  transform: scale(1.4);
  z-index: 50;
  border: 1px white solid;
  background-color: darkgray;

}

.item:hover > .description {
  visibility:visible;
}
```

The description class is initially hidden. We use the pre-line value for the white-space property. This means that sequences of white space are collapsed, and lines are broken at newline characters as necessary to fill line boxes:

```
.description{
  width: var(--icon-width);
  white-space: pre-line;
  visibility:hidden;
}

.descr-text{
  height: 40px;
  display:block;
  overflow: hidden;
  padding: 0 10px;
  text-align: left;
}
```

The description contains small buttons, to play a movie, like it or add it to the user's list. Their icons are also taken from Font Awsome. We use a *flex container* to position the icons in one row:

```css
.descr-buttons-container {
  display: flex;
  flex-direction: row;
  padding: 0 10px;

}

.descr-button {
  display: flex;
  align-items: center;
  justify-content: center;
  width: 20px;
  height: 20px;
  border: 2px solid white;
  text-align: center;
  font-size: 8px;
  margin-right: 5px;
  border-radius: 100%;
}
```

Finally, here is the styling for the next/previous buttons. Note the `absolute` position we talked about earlier. We also give a high `z-index` value to make them appear on top of the slider:

```css
img {
  width: 15rem;
}

.previous,.previous2,
.next, .next2 {
  width: var(--arrow-width);
  height: var(--icon-height);
  border-radius: 5px;
  position: absolute;
  top: 50%;
  background-color: rgba(0, 0, 0, 0.3);
  outline: none;
  border: none;
  color: white;
  z-index: 100;
  cursor: pointer;

}

.next, .next2 {
  right: 0;
}
```

Let's now delve into the JavaScript code:

```javascript
const sliderEl = document.querySelector(".slider");
const slider2El = document.querySelector(".slider2");
const previousEl = document.querySelector(".previous");
const nextEl = document.querySelector(".next");
const previous2El = document.querySelector(".previous2");
const next2El = document.querySelector(".next2");
const IMAGE_PATH = 'https://image.tmdb.org/t/p/w500/';

const URL1 =
'https://api.themoviedb.org/3/discover/movie?include_adult=false&include_video=false&
language=en-US&page=1&sort_by=popularity.desc';
const URL2 = 'https://api.themoviedb.org/3/movie/top_rated';

let sliderPos1 = 0;
let sliderPos2 = 0;
let sliderMax1 = 0;
let sliderMax2 = 0;

const fetchMovies = async (url) => {
  let json;
  try {
    const response = await fetch(url, {
      headers: { Authorization: 'Bearer XXXXXXXX' }
    });
    json = await response.json();
  }
  catch (error) {
    if (error instanceof SyntaxError) {
      alert("The returned data was invalid");
      return null;
    }
    else {
      alert("There was an error with the request");
      return null;
    }
  }
  return json;
}

const slideRight = (e) => {
  let scrollLength = window.innerWidth - 200;
  const sliderTemp =
    e.target.parentElement.parentElement.querySelector('div[class*="slider"]');

  if (e.target.parentNode.classList.contains('next')) {
    if (sliderPos1 - scrollLength > -sliderMax1 + scrollLength)
      sliderPos1 -= scrollLength;
    else
      sliderPos1 = -sliderMax1 + scrollLength;

    sliderTemp.style.transform = `translateX(${sliderPos1}px)`;
  }
```

```javascript
  else {
    if (sliderPos2 - scrollLength > -sliderMax2 + scrollLength)
      sliderPos2 -= scrollLength;
    else
      sliderPos2 = -sliderMax2 + scrollLength;

    sliderTemp.style.transform = `translateX(${sliderPos2}px)`;
  }
}

const slideLeft = (e) => {
  let scrollLength = window.innerWidth - 200;
  const sliderTemp =
e.target.parentElement.parentElement.querySelector('div[class*="slider"]');

  if (e.target.parentNode.classList.contains('previous')) {
    if (sliderPos1 + scrollLength < 0)
      sliderPos1 += scrollLength;
    else
      sliderPos1 = 0;

    sliderTemp.style.transform = `translateX(${sliderPos1}px)`;
  }
  else {
    if (sliderPos2 + scrollLength < 0)
      sliderPos2 += scrollLength;
    else
      sliderPos2 = 0;

    sliderTemp.style.transform = `translateX(${sliderPos2}px)`;
  }
}

const createMovieIcon = (movie) => {
  const img = document.createElement("img");
  img.src = IMAGE_PATH + movie.backdrop_path;

  const description = document.createElement("div");
  description.innerHTML = `<div class="descr-buttons-container">
<div class="descr-button"><i class="fas fa-play"></i></div>
<div class="descr-button"><i class="fas fa-plus"></i></div>
<div class="descr-button"><i class="fas fa-thumbs-up"></i></div>
<div class="descr-button"><i class="fas fa-thumbs-down"></i></div>
<div class="descr-button"><i class="fas fa-chevron-down"></i></div>
</div><div class="descr-text">` + movie.title + "</div>";
  description.classList.add("description");

  const item = document.createElement("div");
  item.classList.add("item");
  item.appendChild(img);
  item.appendChild(description);

  return item;
}
```

```
// Scroll left buttons
previousEl.addEventListener("click", slideLeft);
previous2El.addEventListener("click", slideLeft);

// Scroll right buttons
nextEl.addEventListener("click", slideRight);
next2El.addEventListener("click", slideRight);

fetchMovies(URL1)
  .then((data) => {
    data.results.forEach((movie) => {
      sliderEl.appendChild(createMovieIcon(movie));
    });

    sliderMax1 = data.results.length * 250;
  })
  .catch((e) => {
    alert("the request to the API failed");
  });

fetchMovies(URL2)
  .then((data) => {
    data.results.forEach((movie) => {
      slider2El.appendChild(createMovieIcon(movie));
    })
    sliderMax2 = data.results.length * 250;
  })
  .catch((e) => {
    alert("the request to the API failed");
  });
```

Listing 19-3: script.js

First, we define the fetchMovies() function that will be user to retrieve the movie details from the API. Note that inside the fetch() operation we supply a header with the Authorization property that should contain the API key next to the Bearer keyword.

Next, we define the handlers for the the left and right scrolling of the sliders. Inside the functions we make some calculations about how much the slider should scroll, since we don't want it to scroll too much and leave empty spaces to either side.

We achieve the scolling by modifying the CSS translateX property. This property defines how much the element will shift to the left or to the right (negative values can also be used):

```
sliderTemp.style.transform = `translateX(${sliderPos1}px)`;
```

Next, we define the createMovieIcon() function that returns a <div> element containing the movie icon, title and the respective buttons.

Then, we attach the event listeners to the scroll buttons and, finally, we call function fetchMovies() twice, one for each URL. Since fetchMovies() is asynchronous, and we are at the top level, we will use then() and catch() to handle the Promise. Upon successful completion of the API request, we create the movie items, and we append them to the respective slider.

You can find this project in GitHub:

https://github.com/htset/vanilla_javascript_projects/tree/main/movies

20. Book list with Node.js API

So far, we have worked with ther people's APIs. We can make our own API using Node.js with Express and MongoDB. We will create a simple form that will be used to add and remove books from our database.

Bookstore

Author:

Title:

Number of Pages:

Add Book

Book List

Twenty Thousand Leagues Under the Seas by Jules Verne (324 pages)   Delete

Journey to the Center of the Earth by Jules Verne (411 pages)   Delete

Concepts covered

- Node.js
- RESTful APIs
- MongoDB & Mongoose

Proposed Solution

Our project will consist of two parts, a server-side with Node.js and a client-side with vanilla JavaScript. The project will have the following file structure:

```
project-root/
|-- src/
|    |-- app.js
|
|-- public/
|    |-- index.html
```

```
|    |-- style.css
|    |-- script.js
|
|-- package.json
|-- package-lock.json
```

In the *src* folder we will put file *app.js* with the server-side code. The *public* folder will contain the *index.html* file along with the CSS file and the client-side JavaScript code (*script.js*).

We will first create a new project:

```
npm init
```

Then we will install the necessary libraries from NPM:

```
npm install express body-parser mongoose --save
```

The package.json file that we will use will be like the following:

```
{
  "name": "api",
  "version": "1.0.0",
  "description": "",
  "scripts": {
    "start": "node app"
  },
  "author": "",
  "license": "ISC",
  "dependencies": {
    "body-parser": "^1.20.2",
    "express": "^4.18.2",
    "mongoose": "^8.1.1"
  }
}
```

Listing 20-1: package.json

Note that we have added a *start* script that will run the *app.js* file with Node.

We will use a local instance of *MongoDB* (https://www.mongodb.com) as our database. On top of MongoDB, we will use *Mongoose* (https://mongoosejs.com), a library that helps us model our application data by creating schemas. We can use those schemas to perform validation, make queries on the database and more.

We can use a tool like the *MongoDBCompass* to create new database (books) and a new collection inside the DB (books).

Server-side (Node.js)

On the server-side, we will use the *Express* framework to build the RESTful API with Node.js (https://expressjs.com). Express makes our life easier when we create web applications and APIs with Node.js.

We will start with the server-side API code:

```
const express = require('express');
const bodyParser = require('body-parser');
const mongoose = require('mongoose');
const path = require('path');

const app = express();
const PORT = 3000;

app.use(bodyParser.json());
// Serve static files from the public directory
app.use(express.static(path.join(__dirname, 'public')));

mongoose.connect('mongodb://localhost:27017/books');

// Define a Book model
const Book = mongoose.model('Book', {
  author: String,
  title: String,
  pages: Number
});

// GET all books
app.get('/api/books', async (req, res) => {
  try {
    const books = await Book.find();
    console.log(books);
    res.json(books);
  }
  catch (error) {
    res.status(500).json({ error: error.message });
  }
});

// GET a specific book by ID
app.get('/api/books/:id', async (req, res) => {
  try {
    const book = await Book.findById(req.params.id);
    res.json(book);
  }
  catch (error) {
    res.status(404).json({ error: 'Book not found' });
  }
});

// POST a new book
app.post('/api/books', async (req, res) => {
```

```javascript
  const { author, title, pages } = req.body;
  console.log(req.body);

  try {
    const newBook = new Book({ author, title, pages });
    await newBook.save();
    console.log(newBook);
    res.json(newBook);
  }
  catch (error) {
    res.status(400).json({ error: error.message });
  }
});

// PUT/update a specific book by ID
app.put('/api/books/:id', async (req, res) => {
  try {
    const updatedBook = await
      Book.findByIdAndUpdate(req.params.id, req.body, { new: true });
    res.json(updatedBook);
  }
  catch (error) {
    res.status(404).json({ error: 'Book not found' });
  }
});

// DELETE a specific book by ID
app.delete('/api/books/:id', async (req, res) => {
  try {
    const deletedBook = await Book.findByIdAndDelete(req.params.id);
    if (!deletedBook) {
      return res.status(404).json({ error: 'Book not found' });
    }
    res.json({ message: 'Book deleted successfully' });
  }
  catch (error) {
    res.status(500).json({ error: error.message });
  }
});

// Catch-all route to serve index.html for any other requests
app.get('*', (req, res) => {
  res.sendFile(path.join(__dirname, 'public', 'index.html'));
});

app.listen(PORT, () => {
  console.log(`Server is running on port ${PORT}`);
});
```
Listing 20-2: app.js

First of we create a new instance of the Express middleware:

```javascript
const app = express();
```

Then we add the *body-parser* middleware to Express. This will parse the incoming request bodies before our handlers, available under the `req.body` property.

```
app.use(bodyParser.json());
```

Then, we specify that the static content (like our *index.html* file) will be served from the *public* folder):

```
app.use(express.static(path.join(__dirname, 'public')));
```

Next, we connect to MongoDB, and we create a Mongoose model for the book objects:

```
mongoose.connect('mongodb://localhost:27017/books');

// Define a Book model
const Book = mongoose.model('Book', {
  author: String,
  title: String,
  pages: Number
});
```

Every book object will consist of the book's author, title and number of pages. With Mongoose we can also specify the types of properties, something that can be used for validation.

Next, we define how the GET request should be handled:

```
// GET all books
app.get('/api/books', async (req, res) => {
  try {
    const books = await Book.find();
    console.log(books);
    res.json(books);
  }
  catch (error) {
    res.status(500).json({ error: error.message });
  }
});
```

More specifically, the GET request to the `/api/books` route will be handled by the async arrow function defined here. In this function, we use the Mongoose model to query the MongoDB database and get all the available books. The resulting array sent to the client in an HTTP response containing JSON in its body.

Next, we have the route that request a book with a specific ID:

```
// GET a specific book by ID
app.get('/api/books/:id', async (req, res) => {
```

```
  try {
    const book = await Book.findById(req.params.id);
    res.json(book);
  }
  catch (error) {
    res.status(404).json({ error: 'Book not found' });
  }
});
```

The book ID is contained in the request parameters (`req.params.id`) and is used by Mongoose to retrieve the requested book.

The POST request is used to add new books in the database:

```
// POST a new book
app.post('/api/books', async (req, res) => {
  const { author, title, pages } = req.body;
  console.log(req.body);

  try {
    const newBook = new Book({ author, title, pages });
    await newBook.save();
    console.log(newBook);
    res.json(newBook);
  }
  catch (error) {
    res.status(400).json({ error: error.message });
  }
});
```

The POST request should have the following body structure (in JSON):

```
{
  "author": "Jules Verne",
  "title": "Twenty Thousand Leagues Under the Seas"
  "pages": 324
}
```

In the handler function, we retrieve the book properties from the request body, and we use them to create a new book object with Mongoose. We then save the book in the database, and we return the newly added book in the response body.

The PUT request is used to update an existing book in the database.:

```
// PUT/update a specific book by ID
app.put('/api/books/:id', async (req, res) => {
  try {
    const updatedBook = await
      Book.findByIdAndUpdate(req.params.id, req.body, { new: true });
    res.json(updatedBook);
```

```
  }
  catch (error) {
    res.status(404).json({ error: 'Book not found' });
  }
});
```

We use the ID of the book passed in the request parameters to find the selected book from the database and update it.

Next, the DELETE request is used to find a book and delete it from the database:

```
// DELETE a specific book by ID
app.delete('/api/books/:id', async (req, res) => {
  try {
    const deletedBook = await Book.findByIdAndDelete(req.params.id);
    if (!deletedBook) {
      return res.status(404).json({ error: 'Book not found' });
    }
    res.json({ message: 'Book deleted successfully' });
  }
  catch (error) {
    res.status(500).json({ error: error.message });
  }
});
```

Finally, we create a final route that will handle the rest of the requests (typically requests for static content). We also call listen() in order to wait for incoming requests:

```
// Catch-all route to serve index.html for any other requests
app.get('*', (req, res) => {
  res.sendFile(path.join(__dirname, 'public', 'index.html'));
});

app.listen(PORT, () => {
  console.log(`Server is running on port ${PORT}`);
});
```

When a request arrives at our server, Express tries to match it with a specific route, and the respective handler function is called.

We can start the Node server by running:

```
node app
```

or:

```
npm start
```

We can test the API with a utility like Postman (https://www.postman.com). With Postman we can send RESTful requests to an API and check the response.

Client-side

We will start with the *index.html* file in the *public* folder:

```html
<!DOCTYPE html>
<html lang="en">

<head>
  <meta charset="UTF-8">
  <link rel="stylesheet" type="text/css" href="style.css">
  <title>Bookstore Client</title>
</head>

<body>
  <div class="container">
    <h1>Bookstore</h1>
    <form id="addBookForm">
      <label for="author">Author:</label>
      <input type="text" id="author" required>

      <label for="title">Title:</label>
      <input type="text" id="title" required>

      <label for="pages">Number of Pages:</label>
      <input type="number" id="pages" required>

      <button type="submit">Add Book</button>
    </form>

    <div id="bookList">
      <h2>Book List</h2>
      <ul id="books"></ul>
    </div>
  </div>
  <script src="script.js" type="text/javascript"></script>
</body>

</html>
```

Listing 20-3: index.html

Here, we have a simple form and an empty unordered list.

Let's see now the CSS stylesheet:

```css
body {
  font-family: 'Arial', sans-serif;
  background-color: #f4f4f4;
  margin: 0;
  padding: 0;
}
```

```css
.container {
  max-width: 800px;
  margin: 20px auto;
  background-color: #fff;
  padding: 20px;
  box-shadow: 0 4px 8px rgba(0, 0, 0, 0.1);
}

h1 {
  color: #333;
}

form {
  margin-bottom: 20px;
}

label {
  display: block;
  margin-bottom: 8px;
}

input {
  width: 100%;
  padding: 8px;
  margin-bottom: 16px;
  box-sizing: border-box;
}

button {
  background-color: #007bff;
  color: #fff;
  padding: 10px 20px;
  border: none;
  cursor: pointer;
}

button:hover {
  background-color: #0056b3;
}

#bookList {
  margin-top: 20px;
}

ul {
  list-style-type: none;
  padding: 0;
}

li {
  background-color: #fff;
  padding: 12px;
  margin-bottom: 8px;
```

```css
  box-shadow: 0 2px 4px rgba(0, 0, 0, 0.1);
  display: flex;
  justify-content: space-between;
  align-items: center;
}

button.delete {
  background-color: #dc3545;
  color: #fff;
  padding: 8px;
  border: none;
  cursor: pointer;
}

button.delete:hover {
  background-color: #c82333;
}
```

Listing 20-4: style.css

Now, time for the JS file:

```js
const addBookFormEl = document.getElementById('addBookForm');
const authorInputEl = document.getElementById('author');
const titleInputEl = document.getElementById('title');
const pagesInputEl = document.getElementById('pages');
const booksListEl = document.getElementById('books');

// Fetch all books and display them on the list
async function fetchBooks() {
  const response = await fetch('/api/books');
  const books = await response.json();

  // Clear the existing book list
  booksListEl.innerHTML = '';

  // Fill the book list
  books.forEach(book => {
    const listItem = document.createElement('li');
    listItem.textContent = `${book.title} by ${book.author} (${book.pages} pages)`;

    // Add a delete button
    const deleteButton = document.createElement('button');
    deleteButton.textContent = 'Delete';
    deleteButton.addEventListener('click', async () => {
      // Make a DELETE request to remove the book
      await fetch(`/api/books/${book._id}`, {
        method: 'DELETE',
      });

      // Fetch the updated list of books after deletion
      await fetchBooks();
    });

    listItem.appendChild(deleteButton);
```

```
    booksListEl.appendChild(listItem);
  });
}

// Event haNdler for adding a new book
const submitForm = async (event) => {
  event.preventDefault();

  const author = authorInputEl.value;
  const title = titleInputEl.value;
  const pages = parseInt(pagesInputEl.value);

  // Make a POST request to add a new book
  await fetch('/api/books', {
    method: 'POST',
    headers: {
      'Content-Type': 'application/json',
    },
    body: JSON.stringify({ author, title, pages }),
  });

  // Clear the form and fetch the updated list of books
  addBookFormEl.reset();
  await fetchBooks();
}

addBookFormEl.addEventListener('submit', submitForm);

fetchBooks().then();
```

Listing 20-5: script.js

First, we define the fetchContents() function, that sends a GET request to the API using fetch(). The returned JSON string is parsed, and an array of book objects is created.

We then loop over this array and build the unordered list (<ul>) of books. In each entry, we add a list item (<li>). This item contains the book information and a delete button. When this button is pressed the callback function is called, which sends a DELETE request to the API.

Next, we define a function that will handle the submit event from the form. This function gets the form content and puts it in a POST request using fetch(). The data is transformed into JSON and inserted in the request body. We also specify the content type of the request to be application/json.

Upon completion of this operation, we empty the form contents and we await on the fetchContents() function to update the book list.

Finally, we register the submit event handler and we call the fetchContents() function for the first time. We are at the top-level now, so we cannot use await before the function call.

We can use `await` inside `async` functions. The `fetchContents()` function return a Promise; therefore, we will use `then()`:

```
fetchBooks().then();
```

In this file, we have not included any error handling to make the code more readable. We have seen such error handling in previous projects anyway. In any case, we will have to use `try/catch` when we use `async/await`. Moreover, we should use `catch()` to catch any error with the Promise at the last line of the file.

We can view our project at http://localhost:3000/

You can find this project in GitHub:

https://github.com/htset/vanilla_javascript_projects/tree/main/api

21. Master-detail form (Angular clone)

In this project, we will create a master-detail form where users are presented on a table. When a user is selected, then the detail form is filled with the user's details. When we change the details of the user, the corresponding entry in the table is updated.

We will create this project in a way that resembles how Angular works. This will be a simple example that will demonstrate some of the inner workings of Angular.

Master Component

ID	Name	Email
1	John Doe	john@example.com
2	Jane Doe	jane@example.com
3	Bob Smith	bob@example.com
4	Alice Johnson	alice@example.com
5	Charlie Brown	charlie@example.com
6	Eva Williams	eva@example.com
7	Michael Davis	michael@example.com
8	Olivia Wilson	olivia@example.com
9	James Miller	james@example.com
10	Sophia Moore	sophia@example.com

Detail Component

ID:

```
3
```

Name:

```
Bob Smith
```

Email:

```
bob@example.com
```

Concepts covered

- ES6 Proxies
- Custom events
- bind() function

Proposed Solution

We will start with a simple HTML that only defines a `<div>` element, where the application will be rendered:

```
<!DOCTYPE html>
<html lang="en">
```

```html
<head>
  <meta charset="UTF-8">
  <title>Angular clone</title>
  <link href="style.css" rel="stylesheet" />
</head>

<body>
  <div id="app"></div>

  <script src="masterComponent.js" type="text/javascript"></script>
  <script src="detailComponent.js" type="text/javascript"></script>
  <script src="appComponent.js" type="text/javascript"></script>
  <script src="app.js" type="text/javascript"></script>
</body>

</html>
```

Listing 21-1:index.html

The MasterComponent class displays the users list and is created as an ES6 class:

```javascript
class MasterComponent {
  constructor(users) {
    this.users = users;
    this.selectedId = null;
  }

  setupEventListeners() {
    const userList = document.getElementById('userList');

    userList.addEventListener('click', (event) => {
      const clickedRow = event.target.closest('tr');
      if (clickedRow) {
        this.selectedId = clickedRow.getAttribute('data-user-id');
        // Emit a custom event when form values change
        const ev = new CustomEvent('userSelected', { detail: this.selectedId });
        document.dispatchEvent(ev);
      }
    });
  }

  render() {
    return `
      <div>
        <h2>Master Component</h2>
        <table id="userList">
          <thead>
            <tr>
              <th>ID</th>
              <th>Name</th>
              <th>Email</th>
            </tr>
          </thead>
          <tbody>
```

164

```
        ${this.users.map(user => `
          <tr data-user-id="${user.id}"
            ${(this.selectedId == user.id)? 'class="selected-row"':''}>
            <td>${user.id}</td>
            <td>${user.name}</td>
            <td>${user.email}</td>
          </tr>`).join('')}
        </tbody>
      </table>
    </div>
    `;
  }
}
```

Listing 21-2: masterComponent.js

In the constructor, we define the data that this component will handle: the list of users and the selected user ID.

In the setEventListeners() function we add an event listener for the click event. The event handler finds the row that was clicked on and gets the ID of the selected user from the data-user-id custom attribute. Then, it emits a custom event with the name userSelected, which contains the ID of the selected user.

Finally, the render() function contains a template string that will be used to create the HTML code for this component. Note that the selected row has the selected-row class applied to it.

Next, let's see the detail component:

```
class DetailComponent {
  constructor() {
    this.user = new Proxy({
      id: '',
      name: '',
      email: ''
    }, {
      set: (target, prop, value) => {
        target[prop] = value;
        this.setFormData(this.user);
        return true;
      }
    });
  }

  setupEventListeners() {
    const userForm = document.getElementById('userForm');

    userForm.addEventListener('input', (event) => {
      const formData = new FormData(userForm);
      this.user.id = parseInt(formData.get('userId'));
      this.user.name = formData.get('userName');
      this.user.email = formData.get('userEmail');
```

165

```javascript
      const user = {
        id: parseInt(formData.get('userId')),
        name: formData.get('userName'),
        email: formData.get('userEmail')
      };

      // Emit a custom event when form values change
      const ev = new CustomEvent('formChange', { detail: user });
      document.dispatchEvent(ev);
    });
  }

  render() {
    return `
      <div>
        <h2>Detail Component</h2>
        <form id="userForm">
          <label for="userId">ID:</label>
          <input type="text" id="userId" name="userId"
            value="${this.user.id}" readonly>

          <label for="userName">Name:</label>
          <input type="text" id="userName" name="userName"
            value="${this.user.name}">

          <label for="userEmail">Email:</label>
          <input type="email" id="userEmail" name="userEmail"
            value="${this.user.email}">
        </form>
      </div>
      `;
  }

  setFormData(user) {
    const userIdField = document.getElementById('userId');
    const userNameField = document.getElementById('userName');
    const userEmailField = document.getElementById('userEmail');

    userIdField.value = user.id;
    userNameField.value = user.name;
    userEmailField.value = user.email;
  }
}
```

Listing 21-3: detailComponent.js

In the DetailComponent class we have a form that displays the user's data. Note that the ID form field is `readonly`, as we do not want to have this changed.

This component uses *two-way binding*; this means that there is a two-way connection between the user object and the corresponding form fields. When the data in the form is changed, then the object is updated. Respectively, when the user object is changed, then the contents of the form fields are updated to reflect the change.

The former is achieved by listening for the input event on the form. When this event is fired, then the user object is updated.

The latter is performed with the use of *ES6 Proxies*. A *Proxy* is an object that wraps another object and traps certain operations on this object. Here, we define the set() trap: when a property of the user object is modified, then the set() trap of the Proxy is invoked and calls the setFormData() function. As a result, the form fields are automatically updated.

Moreover, when a form field is modified, another custom event (formChange) is emitted, containing the modified user data.

Next, let's see AppComponent, the top-level component that contains the other two objects:

```
class AppComponent {
  constructor(users) {
    this.users = users;

    this.masterComponent = new MasterComponent(this.users);
    this.detailComponent = new DetailComponent();

    this.init();
  }

  init() {
    this.render();
    document.addEventListener('formChange', this.handleFormChange.bind(this));
    document.addEventListener('userSelected', this.handleUserSelected.bind(this));
  }

  handleFormChange(event) {
    const user = event.detail;
    console.log(`Form change event received for user with ID ${user.id}`);
    console.log('Form data:', user);

    const userIndex = this.users.findIndex(u => u.id === user.id);
    if (userIndex !== -1) {
      this.users[userIndex] = user;
    }

    this.render();
  }

  handleUserSelected(event) {
    const userId = event.detail;
    console.log(`User selected event received for user with ID ${userId}`);
    const user = this.users.find(u => u.id === parseInt(userId));

    this.render();
```

```
    if(user != null){
      this.detailComponent.user.id = user.id;
      this.detailComponent.user.name = user.name;
      this.detailComponent.user.email = user.email;
    }
  }

  render() {
    const appElement = document.getElementById('app');
    appElement.innerHTML         =         this.masterComponent.render()         +
this.detailComponent.render();
    this.masterComponent.setupEventListeners();
    this.detailComponent.setupEventListeners();
  }
}
```

Listing 21-4: appComponent.js

In the constructor, AppComponent creates the two child components and renders them on the only <div> element of the web app.

AppComponent also defines event handlers for the two custom events emited by the child components. In handleFormChange() we get the modified user data and we update the users list. Then we proceed with rendering the components. In handleUserSelected() we get the selected user data from the list and we populate the detail form. Note the find() and findIndex() functions of the array prototype; we are using array functions to find the searched user inside the array.

In the init() function, note that we bind the two event handles to the AppComponent object using the bind() function. If we forget to use bind(), then the this object inside the handlers will be null.

Finally, let's see the entry point, the *app.js* file:

```
const users = [
  { id: 1, name: 'John Doe', email: 'john@example.com' },
  { id: 2, name: 'Jane Doe', email: 'jane@example.com' },
  { id: 3, name: 'Bob Smith', email: 'bob@example.com' },
  { id: 4, name: 'Alice Johnson', email: 'alice@example.com' },
  { id: 5, name: 'Charlie Brown', email: 'charlie@example.com' },
  { id: 6, name: 'Eva Williams', email: 'eva@example.com' },
  { id: 7, name: 'Michael Davis', email: 'michael@example.com' },
  { id: 8, name: 'Olivia Wilson', email: 'olivia@example.com' },
  { id: 9, name: 'James Miller', email: 'james@example.com' },
  { id: 10, name: 'Sophia Moore', email: 'sophia@example.com' },
];

const app = new AppComponent(users);
```

Listing 21-5: app.js

Here, we define the list of users as an array, and we pass it as argument to the created `AppComponent` object. Then we attach event listeners to the two custom events fired by the child components.

This is a very simple example, mainly to show how the components are structured and how two-way binding works. Angular is a very complex system with loads of features that cannot be covered in such a small example.

You can find this project in GitHub:

https://github.com/htset/vanilla_javascript_projects/tree/main/angularClone

22. Master-detail form (React clone)

In this project, we will modify the master-detail form of the previous example, so that it can demonstrate some of the inner workings of React.

ID	Name	Email		ID:
				1
2	Jane Doe	jane@example.com		Name:
3	Bob Smith	bob@example.com		John Doe
4	Alice Johnson	alice@example.com		Email:
5	Charlie Brown	charlie@example.com		john@example.con
6	Eva Williams	eva@example.com		
7	Michael Davis	michael@example.com		
8	Olivia Wilson	olivia@example.com		
9	James Miller	james@example.com		
10	Sophia Moore	sophia@example.com		

Concepts covered

- Functional components

Proposed Solution

We will start with a same HTML file:

```
<!DOCTYPE html>
<html lang="en">

<head>
  <meta charset="UTF-8">
  <title>React clone</title>
  <link href="style.css" rel="stylesheet" />
</head>

<body>
  <div id="app"></div>

  <script src="masterComponent.js" type="text/javascript"></script>
```

```
  <script src="detailComponent.js" type="text/javascript"></script>
  <script src="appComponent.js" type="text/javascript"></script>
  <script src="app.js" type="text/javascript"></script>
</body>

</html>
```

Listing 22-1:index.html

Modern React uses functional components instead of classes, and this is what we will do too:

```
function MasterComponent(users, selectedUser, onSelectUser) {
  const table = document.createElement('table');
  const thead = document.createElement('thead');
  const tbody = document.createElement('tbody');

  thead.innerHTML = '<tr><th>ID</th><th>Name</th><th>Email</th></tr>';
  table.appendChild(thead);
  table.appendChild(tbody);

  function render() {
    // Clear the tbody before updating
    tbody.innerHTML = '';

    users.forEach(user => {
      const row = document.createElement('tr');
      row.setAttribute('data-user-id', user.id);

      const idCell = document.createElement('td');
      idCell.textContent = user.id;

      const nameCell = document.createElement('td');
      nameCell.textContent = user.name;

      const emailCell = document.createElement('td');
      emailCell.textContent = user.email;

      row.appendChild(idCell);
      row.appendChild(nameCell);
      row.appendChild(emailCell);

      if (selectedUser != null && user.id == selectedUser.id) {
        row.classList.add('selected-row');
      }

      tbody.appendChild(row);
    });

    return table;
  }

  table.addEventListener('click', (event) => {
    const targetRow = event.target.closest('tr[data-user-id]');
```

172

```
  if (targetRow) {
    selectedUserId = parseInt(targetRow.getAttribute('data-user-id'), 10);
    onSelectUser(selectedUserId);
  }
});

  return { render };
}
```
Listing 22-2: masterComponent.js

We create the MasterComponent() function that takes as arguments:

- The users list
- The selectedUser object
- The reference to a function (onSelectUser)

The former two objects are used in the render() function that creates and populates the `<table>` element. React uses *JSX code* to define the component template. The JSX code is then transformed by *Babel* into JavaScript code like the one in our example.

The onSelectUser function is supplied by the parent object and is used as a handler for the click event. When the user clicks on the table, then the closest table row is determined, and the corresponding user ID is found. Then, we call the supplied function with the user ID as parameter.

Finally, MasterComponent() function return the reference to the render() function; this will be called by the parent element when there is need to refresh the list.

Let's now examine the detail component:

```
function DetailComponent(selectedUser, onUpdateUser) {
  const detailComponent = document.createElement('div');

  function render() {
    detailComponent.innerHTML = selectedUser
      ? `
        <form id="userForm">
          <label for="userName">ID:</label>
          <input type="text" id="userId" name="id"
            value="${selectedUser.id}" readonly/>

          <label for="userName">Name:</label>
          <input type="text" id="userName" name="name"
           value="${selectedUser.name}" />

          <label for="userEmail">Email:</label>
          <input type="email" id="userEmail" name="email"
            value="${selectedUser.email}" />
        </form>
      `
      : '<div>No user selected</div>';
```

```
    return detailComponent;
  }

  detailComponent.addEventListener('input', (event) => {
    const userForm = document.getElementById('userForm');
    const formData = new FormData(userForm);
    const newUser = {
      id: parseInt(formData.get('id')),
      name: formData.get('name'),
      email: formData.get('email')
    };

    onUpdateUser(newUser);
  });

  return { render };
}
```

Listing 22-3: detailComponent.js

The `DetailComponent()` function follows the same structure. It defines a `render()` function that uses string templates to build the user data form. Moreover, it registers an event listener for the `input` event. In the event handler, we get the resulting form data and we use it to call function `onUpdateUser()` that is supplied by the parent component as argument in the `DetailComponent()` function.

Next, let's see `AppComponent`, the top-level component:

```
function AppComponent(users, selectedUser) {
  const appElement = document.getElementById('app');
  const masterComponent = MasterComponent(users, selectedUser, onSelectUser);
  const detailComponent = DetailComponent(selectedUser, onUpdateUser);

  function onSelectUser(userId) {
    let user = users.find(user => user.id === userId);
    selectedUser.id = user.id;
    selectedUser.name = user.name;
    selectedUser.email = user.email;

    render();
  }

  function onUpdateUser(updatedUser){
    let user = users.find(user => user.id === updatedUser.id);
    user.name = updatedUser.name;
    user.email = updatedUser.email;

    selectedUser.name = updatedUser.name;
    selectedUser.email = updatedUser.email;

    render();
  }
```

```
  function render() {
    appElement.innerHTML = '';
    appElement.appendChild(masterComponent.render());
    appElement.appendChild(detailComponent.render());
  }

  return { render };
}
```

Listing 22-4: appComponent.js

AppComponent creates the two child components and renders them on the only `<div>` element of the web app.

In the function definition, it gets as parameters the list of users and the currently selected user. This is the *application state* (defined in *app.js*, as we will see later) that is passed as *props* down the component hierarchy. Every time the application state changes, then we render the component tree again to reflect the changes in the UI, just like React does.

AppComponent also defines the two event handlers that are called by the child components. onSelectUser() finds the currently selected user and updates the selectedUser state object. onUpdateUser() gets the modified user object and updates the state accordingly.

Finally, let's see the entry point, the *app.js* file:

```
const users = [
  { id: 1, name: 'John Doe', email: 'john@example.com' },
  { id: 2, name: 'Jane Doe', email: 'jane@example.com' },
  { id: 3, name: 'Bob Smith', email: 'bob@example.com' },
  { id: 4, name: 'Alice Johnson', email: 'alice@example.com' },
  { id: 5, name: 'Charlie Brown', email: 'charlie@example.com' },
  { id: 6, name: 'Eva Williams', email: 'eva@example.com' },
  { id: 7, name: 'Michael Davis', email: 'michael@example.com' },
  { id: 8, name: 'Olivia Wilson', email: 'olivia@example.com' },
  { id: 9, name: 'James Miller', email: 'james@example.com' },
  { id: 10, name: 'Sophia Moore', email: 'sophia@example.com' },
];

const selectedUser = { id: 1, name: 'John Doe', email: 'john@example.com' };

const appComponent = AppComponent(users, selectedUser);
appComponent.render();
```

Listing 22-5: app.js

Here, we define the list of users as an array, and we pass it as argument to the created AppComponent() function.

Again, this is a very simple example, mainly to show React uses functions to create components and how the application state is passed from parent to child, triggering rendering.

You can find this project in GitHub:

https://github.com/htset/vanilla_javascript_projects/tree/main/reactClone

23. PacMan game

In this project, we will create a simplified PacMan game.

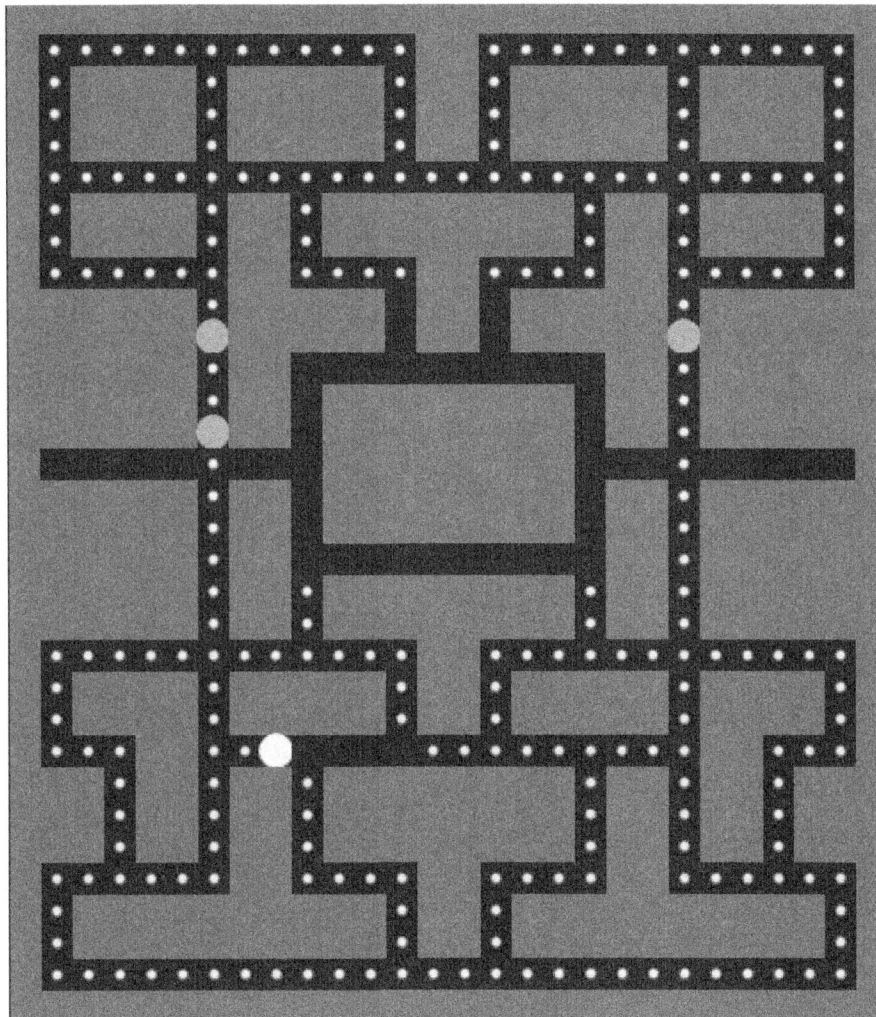

- Drawing on <canvas>
- Game dynamics

Proposed Solution

We will start with a simple HTML file:

```
<!DOCTYPE html>
<html lang="en">
<head>
    <meta charset="UTF-8">
    <meta name="viewport" content="width=device-width, initial-scale=1.0">
    <style>
        canvas {
            border: 1px solid #000;
```

```
        }
    </style>
    <title>Pacman Game</title>
</head>
<body>
    <canvas id="pacmanCanvas" width="560" height="640"></canvas>

    <script src="consts.js"></script>
    <script src="entity.js"></script>
    <script src="pacman.js"></script>
    <script src="ghost.js"></script>
    <script src="game.js"></script>
    <script src="app.js"></script>
</body>
</html>
```

Listing 23-1:index.html

PacMan and the Ghosts possess similar characteristics: the most important is their position in the maze. Moreover, they both need to have access to the maze so that they can find out where they can move to.

With this in mind, we define a base class called Entity:

```
class Entity {
  constructor() {
    this.x = 0;
    this.y = 0;
    this.direction = "left";
    this.type = null;
    this.game = null;
  }

  move(newX, newY) {
    game.map[newX][newY].entity = game.map[this.x][this.y].entity;
    game.map[this.x][this.y].entity = null;
    this.x = newX;
    this.y = newY;
  }
}
```

Listing 23-2: entity.js

In this class, we define the position (parameters x and y), the direction the entity is moving to, its type (pacman or ghost) and a reference to the Game object. The Entity class also defines one method called move() that is used to move an entity inside the map.

Now, let's see the heart of the program, the Game class:

```
class Block {
  constructor(type, entity) {
    history.type = type;
    this.entity = entity;
```

178

```
    }
}

class Game {
  constructor() {
    this.map = [];
    this.sizeX = 32;
    this.sizeY = 28;
    this.gameActive = true;
    this.pacmanLocation = null;
    this.pointsLeft = 0;
    this.player = [];

    // Construct maze
    for (let i = 0; i < 32; i++) {
      let line = matrix[i];
      this.map[i] = [];

      for (let j = 0; j < 28; j++) {
        this.map[i].push(new Block());

        this.map[i][j].entity = null;

        if (line[j] == '.') {
          this.map[i][j].type = "point";
          this.pointsLeft++;
        }
        else if (line[j] == '*')
          this.map[i][j].type = "wall";
        if (line[j] == ' ')
          this.map[i][j].type = "empty";
      }
    }

    // Create players
    this.player.push(new PacMan(this, 23, 13));
    this.map[23][13].entity = this.player[0];
    this.pacmanLocation = { x: 23, y: 13 };

    this.player.push(new Ghost(this, 5, 5));
    this.map[5][5].entity = this.player[1];

    this.player.push(new Ghost(this, 5, 20));
    this.map[5][20].entity = this.player[2];

    this.player.push(new Ghost(this, 8, 5));
    this.map[8][5].entity = this.player[3];
  }

  // Update pacman's direction
  keyPressed(key) {
    console.log("Key pressed: " + key);
    this.player[0].direction = key;
  }
```

```javascript
    // Play round on every tick
    playRound() {
      for (let i = 0; i < 4; i++)
      this.player[i].play();
    }
}
```

The map consists of Block objects. Each Block can be of specific type:

- A wall
- A space with a point
- An empty space

Entities can move to spaces, either empty or with points. When an entity moves to a block, then the entity reference inside the Block object will be set to point to the entity object. Also, each Entity can move to a specific direction.

During the construction of the Game object, we parse an array of strings that make up a text representation of the maze. We also keep track of the remaining points in the game (variable pointsLeft). Finally, we create the game entities, and we place them at their initial positions in the maze.

Note how the newly created entities are placed in the map. This means that we have a bidirectional relationship between the map and the entities, as each object has a reference to the other.

Here is the string array used to initialize the game map:

```
const matrix =
  [
    "*************************",
    "*.............**.............*",
    "*.****.*****.**.*****.****.*",
    "*.****.*****.**.*****.****.*",
    "*.****.*****.**.*****.****.*",
    "*...........................*",
    "*.****.**.********.**.****.*",
    "*.****.**.********.**.****.*",
    "*......**....**....**......*",
    "******.*****.**.*****.******",
    "******.*****.**.*****.******",
    "******.**          **.******",
    "******.**.********.**.******",
    "******.**.********.**.******",
    "*     .   ********   .     *",
    "******.**.********.**.******",
    "******.**.********.**.******",
    "******.**          **.******",
```

```
  "******.**.********.**.******",
  "******.**.********.**.******",
  "*............**............*",
  "*.****.*****.**.*****.****.*",
  "*.****.*****.**.*****.****.*",
  "*...**................**...*",
  "***.**.**.********.**.**.***",
  "***.**.**.********.**.**.***",
  "***.**.**.********.**.**.***",
  "*......**....**....**......*",
  "*.**********.**.**********.*",
  "*.**********.**.**********.*",
  "*.........................*",
  "****************************"
];
```

The asterisks denote a wall, while the dots represent spaces with points. Finally, there are some empty spaces denoted with the space symbol.

The keyPressed() method gets the key code that was pressed and changes the direction of PacMan.

Finally, the play() method is called during every loop and carries out the calculation of the entities' moves.

Speaking about the loop, let's see its implementation in the *app.js* file:

```
class UI {
  static canvas = document.getElementById('pacmanCanvas');
  static context = this.canvas.getContext('2d');

  static draw(game) {
    // Clear all
    this.context.clearRect(0, 0, this.canvas.width, this.canvas.height);

    for (let i = 0; i < 32; i++) {
      for (let j = 0; j < 28; j++) {
        if (game.map[i][j].entity != null) {
          if (game.map[i][j].entity.type == "pacman") {
            // Draw pacman
            this.context.fillStyle = '#000000'; // background
            this.context.fillRect(j * 20, i * 20, 20, 20);
            this.context.fillStyle = '#FFD700'; //pacman
            this.context.beginPath();
            this.context.arc(game.map[i][j].entity.y * 20 + 10,
              game.map[i][j].entity.x * 20 + 10, 11, 0, 2 * Math.PI);
            this.context.closePath();
            this.context.fill();
          }
          else {
            // Draw ghosts
            this.context.fillStyle = '#000000';
            this.context.fillRect(j * 20, i * 20, 20, 20);
```

```javascript
                this.context.fillStyle = '#FF0000';
                this.context.beginPath();
                this.context.arc(game.map[i][j].entity.y * 20 + 10,
                  game.map[i][j].entity.x * 20 + 10, 11, 0, 2 * Math.PI);
                this.context.closePath();
                this.context.fill();
              }
            }
          else if (game.map[i][j].type == "wall") {
            this.context.fillStyle = '#0000FF';
            this.context.fillRect(j * 20, i * 20, 20, 20);
          }
          else if (game.map[i][j].type == "point") {
            this.context.fillStyle = '#000000';
            this.context.fillRect(j * 20, i * 20, 20, 20);
            this.context.fillStyle = '#ebcf34';
            this.context.beginPath();
            this.context.arc(j * 20 + 10, i * 20 + 10, 3, 0, 2 * Math.PI);
            this.context.closePath();
            this.context.fill();
          }
          else if (game.map[i][j].type == "empty") {
            this.context.fillStyle = '#000000';
            this.context.fillRect(j * 20, i * 20, 20, 20);
          }
        }
      }

    if (!game.gameActive) {
      this.context.font = "34px serif";
      this.context.fillStyle = "#ff0000";
      this.context.fillText("Game over", 205, 300);
    }
  }

  static handleUserInput(game) {
    document.addEventListener('keydown', (event) => {
      switch (event.key) {
        case 'ArrowUp':
          game.keyPressed("up");
          break;
        case 'ArrowDown':
          game.keyPressed("down");
          break;
        case 'ArrowLeft':
          game.keyPressed("left");
          break;
        case 'ArrowRight':
          game.keyPressed("right");
          break;
      }
    });
  }
}
```

```
function gameLoop() {
  game.playRound();
  UI.draw(game);
  if (!game.gameActive)
    clearInterval(timerId);
}

const game = new Game();
UI.handleUserInput(game);
let timerId = setInterval(gameLoop, 200);
```

We see that we create a class called UI that will handle the drawing on the canvas. Inside the class, we define two static functions.

In the draw() function, over a black background, we use blue to paint the walls, yellow to paint the points. We also use yellow for PacMan and red for the ghosts (over a black background too).

In the handleUserInput() function we set an event listener for the keydown event. This function passes the selected key to the game object.

Outside of the class we define the gameLoop() function. This function is passed as callback to the setInterval() function, that ticks every 200 ms. On every tick, we play a round and all new positions of the pacman and the ghosts are calculated. Then, the new positions are drawn on the canvas.

The game will end when a ghost catches pacman, or when all points have been collected. In both cases, the timer is stopped and the game ends.

Now, let's see the PacMan class definition:

```
class PacMan extends Entity {
  constructor(map, x, y) {
    super();
    this.game = map;
    this.type = "pacman";
    this.x = x;
    this.y = y;
  }

  play() {
    // Find the neighboring blocks that pacman can move to
    let candidateBlocks = [];
    for (let i = this.x - 1; i <= this.x + 1; i++) {
      for (let j = this.y - 1; j <= this.y + 1; j++) {
        if (i >= 0 && i < game.sizeX
          && j >= 0 && j < game.sizeY
          && !(i == this.x && j == this.y)
          && game.map[i][j].type != "wall") {
```

```
          candidateBlocks.push({ x: i, y: j });
        }
      }
    }

    // Move to a block according to pacman's direction
    if (this.direction == "up"
      && (candidateBlocks
        .find(p => (p.x == this.x - 1 && p.y == this.y))) != null) {
      if (game.map[this.x - 1][this.y].entity != null)
        game.gameActive = false;
      this.move(this.x - 1, this.y);
    }
    else if (this.direction == "right"
      && (candidateBlocks
        .find(p => (p.x == this.x && p.y == this.y + 1))) != null) {
      if (game.map[this.x][this.y + 1].entity != null)
        game.gameActive = false;
      this.move(this.x, this.y + 1);
    }
    else if (this.direction == "down"
      && (candidateBlocks
        .find(p => (p.x == this.x + 1 && p.y == this.y))) != null) {
      if (game.map[this.x + 1][this.y].entity != null)
        game.gameActive = false;
      this.move(this.x + 1, this.y);
    }
    else if (this.direction == "left"
      && (candidateBlocks
        .find(p => (p.x == this.x && p.y == this.y - 1))) != null) {
      if (game.map[this.x][this.y - 1].entity != null)
        game.gameActive = false;
      this.move(this.x, this.y - 1);
    }

    // Update pacman location
    game.pacmanLocation.x = this.x;
    game.pacmanLocation.y = this.y;

    // Pick up point - remove it from the maze
    if (game.map[this.x][this.y].type == "point") {
      game.map[this.x][this.y].type = "empty";
      game.pointsLeft--;
      if (game.pointsLeft == 0)
        game.gameActive = false;
    }
  }
}
```
Listing 23-6: pacman.js

The important stuff lies in the implementation of the play() method. First of all, we find all neighbouring blocks that PacMan can move (those that are not a wall actually) and we put them in a list of candidate blocks.

Next, depending on the `direction` currently selected by the user (using the arrow buttons) we move PacMan into the respective block, if available. Moving PacMan into a block means also updating the map with the position of PacMan, as well the elimination of the point (if any) in this block. The latter is performed by changing the type of the block to `empty` and by reducing by one the remaining points in the game. If the points become zero, then the game comes to an end.

Now let's move to the `Ghost` definition:

```
class Ghost extends Entity {
  constructor(map, x, y) {
    super();
    this.game = map;
    this.type = "ghost";
    this.x = x;
    this.y = y;
  }

  play() {
    // Neighboring block to move to
    let candidateBlocks = [];
    // Distance to pacman from the respective neighbor block
    let distanceToPacman = [];

    for (let i = this.x - 1; i <= this.x + 1; i++)
      for (let j = this.y - 1; j <= this.y + 1; j++) {
        if (i >= 0 && i < game.sizeX
          && j >= 0 && j < game.sizeY
          && !(i == this.x && j == this.y)
          && game.map[i][j].type != "wall") {
          candidateBlocks.push({ x: i, y: j });
          distanceToPacman
            .push(Math.sqrt(Math.pow(i - game.pacmanLocation.x, 2)
              + Math.pow(j - game.pacmanLocation.y, 2)));
        }
      }

    // Get block with the minimum distance to pacman
    let minDistIn = distanceToPacman.indexOf(Math.min(...distanceToPacman));

    if (game.map[candidateBlocks[minDistIn].x][candidateBlocks[minDistIn].y]
        .entity != null) {
      //move only if pacman is there
      if (game.map[candidateBlocks[minDistIn].x][candidateBlocks[minDistIn].y]
          .entity.type == "pacman") {
        //eat pacman
        game.map[candidateBlocks[minDistIn].x][candidateBlocks[minDistIn].y]
          .entity = null;
        game.gameActive = false;
        this.move(candidateBlocks[minDistIn].x, candidateBlocks[minDistIn].y);
      }
    }
    else {
```

```
            this.move(candidateBlocks[minDistIn].x, candidateBlocks[minDistIn].y);
        }
    }
}
```

Listing 23-7: ghost.js

In the `play()` method, we again find the candidate neighbouring blocks for a move. Moreover, we calculate an array of the straight-line distances of each candidate position to the PacMan entity.

After we have calculated the block with the smaller distance, the Ghost will move to this block, in an effort to get closer to PacMan. A Ghost may not move in a block where there is another Ghost, but it can step into the block where PacMan is located. In this case, PacMan is caught by the Ghost and the game comes to an end.

Note the separation between the game logic and the UI. The former is included in the Game, PacMan and Ghost classes, while the latter can be found in the UI class. In this way, it would be easy to test the logic of the game.

This game has definitively lots more to be done. For instance, we have to implement the mode change where PacMan swallows the big pills and starts chasing the Ghosts for a short period of time. Such functionality is left to reader as an exercise.

You can find this project in GitHub:

https://github.com/htset/vanilla_javascript_projects/tree/main/pacman

Printed in Great Britain
by Amazon

50043595R00104